PRISONERS WITHOUT A VOICE

Asylum-seekers detained in the United Kingdom

Second Revised and Updated Edition

Amnesty International British Section

London

ISBN: 1873328117
First published October 1994, this revised and expanded edition published May 1995.

Amnesty International British Section
99-119 Rosebery Avenue
London EC1R 4RE

This report was written and researched by Richard Dunstan of the Refugee Office, Amnesty International British Section.

The author wishes to acknowledge with thanks those individuals and organisations who provided the information on which this report was based.

Designed and printed by Ennisfield Print and Design

CONTENTS

INTRODUCTION

At any one time, some 600 men and women seeking asylum in the United Kingdom are held in detention pending a decision on their asylum claim by the Home Office or the Immigration Appeals Authority. All are held, under general provisions of the Immigration Act 1971, on the basis of a cursory examination by an Immigration Officer, acting without effective reference or accountability to any court or independent review body. While most are held in one of three immigration detention centres, over 200 are held in criminal prisons or police station cells.

Few if any of the detainees have been adequately informed of the specific reasons for their detention and, unlike criminal remand prisoners, many have no right to seek bail. Moreover, even those with a right to seek bail are unlikely to exercise it, simply because they are unable to provide the £4,000 or more of bail guarantees that are invariably demanded. There is no legal limit to the length of such detention.

As a result of this practice, many asylum-seekers have spent months in confinement without proper explanation and without any independent scrutiny of their situation, and it is not surprising that this has led to intense levels of frustration, anxiety and resentment. In February to April 1994 this was expressed in a wave of hunger-strikes by over 200 asylum-seekers in detention centres and prisons throughout the country, and in June 1994 more than 150 police officers were needed to suppress a roof-top demonstration by asylum-seekers held in Campsfield House immigration detention centre, near Oxford.

This practice - or malpractice - is not new. Asylum-seekers have been detained under Immigration Act powers in significant numbers since the mid-1980s, and in 1987 the Home Office even experimented with the use of a converted car ferry to hold over 100 detainees, mostly Sri Lankan Tamils, in Harwich harbour. This experiment was dramatically ended by the violent storm of October 1987, when the ferry broke free of its moorings and began to sink. Similarly, in 1990 a pattern of detentions of Turkish Kurds was abruptly ended by the self-immolation and subsequent death of one detainee. However, the number of asylum-seekers held in detention at any one time has doubled since July 1993, when new, accelerated asylum procedures (established under the Asylum and Immigration Appeals Act 1993) came into force.

Amnesty International has long argued[1] that such practice is in violation of international human rights standards, such as Article 5 of the European Convention on Human Rights, Article 9 of the International Covenant on Civil and Political Rights, the UN Body of Principles for the Protection of All Persons Under Any Form of Detention or Imprisonment, and recommendations of the intergovernmental Executive Committee of the UN High Commission for Refugees (UNHCR).

These standards clearly provide that, in view of the hardship which it involves, the detention of asylum-seekers should be avoided and resorted to only for certain, specified reasons. They also provide that, in the exceptional event that it is necessary to detain an asylum-seeker, the detainee should be fully informed of the specific reasons for detention and of his or her rights, should be able to challenge those reasons at a *prompt*, and *automatic*, hearing before an independent review body, and should be held in facilities appropriate to his or her status, not with people who have been charged or convicted of a criminal offence.

---

[1] See Appendix 3 for information on Amnesty International's previous work on this issue.

In response, the Government has repeatedly rejected any suggestion that its detention policy is in breach of its international obligations. It has defended its policy and practice by claiming that "only a very small proportion of asylum-seekers is detained", and by implying that those in detention are not genuine refugees. It has argued that detention is used "only as a last resort" in those cases where, in the view of the Immigration Officer, the applicant would otherwise abscond, and that internal Immigration Service reviews and the opportunity to apply to the Immigration Appeals Authority (IAA) or the courts for bail provide "adequate safeguards to ensure the proper application of this policy".

It is certainly the case that most of those applying for asylum in the United Kingdom are not detained for any length of time, but are granted temporary admission while their asylum claim is examined by the Home Office. Indeed, the number of asylum-seekers in detention at any one time (eg 619 on 29 March 1995) represents less than 1.5% of the total number of applications under active consideration by the Home Office (56,000 in February 1995). It is therefore apparent that the authorities are able to deal with over 98.5% of all asylum cases *without* having to resort to detention and, seemingly, without any significant problem of rejected applicants absconding before they can be expelled.[2] The essential issue, therefore, is that of why some individuals are detained when so many others are not. Amnesty International has long suspected that decisions to detain are in many cases arbitrary, dependent more upon factors such as the availability of detention places on any given day and individual Immigration Officers' attitudes towards refugees, than on an objective and considered assessment of whether detention is actually necessary.

---

[2] Despite repeated requests from Amnesty International and others, ministers have failed to produce any statistical evidence to support their claim that the number of asylum-seekers granted temporary admission who subsequently abscond is a "serious problem" justifying existing detention policy. See also *Some basic findings and general remarks*, below.

Immigration officers make decisions to detain without reference or effective accountability to any court or independent review body. There is no requirement, as there is in the case of someone arrested by the police and charged with a criminal offence, for the detainee to be brought before a court within a fixed time period, or indeed at any time. As a result, the decision to detain is not subject to any independent scrutiny and there is no reliable means of establishing that it is both right and fair.

In July 1993, Amnesty International decided to test the Government's defence of its detention policy by monitoring the cases of 50 detained asylum-seekers. In particular, the organisation set out to establish whether or not in each case the detainee was: a) adequately informed of the specific reasons for his or her detention, and of his or her rights and how to exercise them; b) able to challenge those reasons promptly and effectively before an independent review body; and c) held in appropriate accommodation.

The cases were drawn at random from among the caseloads of over 20 different legal representatives, and included detainees of 24 different nationalities (see Appendix 1 for summarised case histories of the 50 detainees). All the detainees concerned, 44 men and six women, applied for asylum after 26 July 1993, and their cases were therefore dealt with under the new asylum procedures established by the Asylum and Immigration Appeals Act 1993, which the Government had claimed would "enable asylum claims to be settled more quickly, with shorter periods of detention on average". All were detained from the time of application for asylum, and in each case the intention was to monitor the situation of the detainee until his or her asylum claim was fully resolved.

This report, first published on 18 October 1994, sets out the findings of that study, together with Amnesty International's recommendations to the Government. This edition, revised and updated to take account of new information available up to 31 March 1995, also incorporates Amnesty International's comments on the Government's response to the original report.

SOME ESSENTIAL BACKGROUND

The asylum procedures

Each year some 20,000 - 30,000 people seek asylum in the United Kingdom. As a party to the 1951 UN Convention on Refugees, the Government is legally obliged to offer protection to any asylum-seeker who can demonstrate a "well-founded fear of being persecuted for reasons of race, religion, nationality, membership of a particular social group, or political opinion" (Article 1). Clearly, this obligation demands the existence of an effective process of determining between those asylum-seekers who qualify as refugees, and those who do not.

All applications for asylum are considered and determined by officials in the Asylum Division of the Home Office's Immigration and Nationality Department (IND), which has stated that applications are "considered against the criteria of the [1951 UN] Convention and with the help of guidance and information from a wide range of sources". However, the procedures vary according to whether the application is made upon arrival at a port, or after entry to the United Kingdom.

In those cases where, at the time of applying for asylum, the applicant has permission to be in the United Kingdom on another basis, eg as a visitor or as a student, he or she is normally given an Asylum Questionnaire for self-completion and return within four weeks and, subsequently, interviewed by an Asylum Division official. Such applicants are rarely, if ever, detained (but see also *The legal basis for detention* below).

In other cases, however, the initial examination and interview of the applicant is carried out by an Immigration Officer (based at a port), and the results of this examination and interview are then passed to the Asylum Division for determination of the asylum application. These include: a) cases where the application is made at immigration control upon arrival at an airport or seaport ("port" cases); b) cases where the applicant has been deemed to be an "illegal entrant", eg where the applicant has applied for asylum after legal entry to the United Kingdom on another basis, but only after that original permission to be in the country has expired, or where the applicant has been apprehended after entering, or attempting to enter, the country using forged documents (or without documents) and has then applied for asylum ("illegal entrant" cases); and c) the small number of cases where, at the time the asylum application is made, the applicant is already the subject of deportation action on other grounds, eg following conviction of a criminal offence and a court recommendation for deportation[3] ("deportation" cases). It is in these categories of cases that the applicant is liable to detention pending the determination of his or her asylum claim (see also *The legal basis for detention* below).

If, having considered the application and any representations or further information submitted by the applicant's legal representative, the Asylum Division is satisfied that the applicant qualifies as a refugee under the 1951 UN Convention, he or she will be granted asylum. If the Asylum Division is not so satisfied, but accepts that there are strong "humanitarian or compassionate" reasons why the applicant should be allowed to remain in the United Kingdom, then he or she may be granted Exceptional Leave to Remain (ELR).[4] If the Asylum Division is not satisfied that the applicant qualifies for either asylum or ELR, then the application will be refused.

---

[3] The 1971 Immigration Act provides for a recommendation for deportation as part of the sentence after a conviction for an imprisonable offence, if the defendant has no right of abode in the UK.

[4] Asylum is granted for a period of four years, after which Indefinite Leave to Remain may be applied for (and is invariably granted). ELR is granted for 12 months initially and then (subject to renewal) for two further periods of three years, after which Indefinite Leave to Remain may be applied for. Unlike those granted asylum, applicants granted ELR have no right to family reunion or to a UN refugee travel document. Since July 1993 the Home Office's use of ELR has declined markedly, despite there being no apparent change in the nature of application.

Moreover, if the applicant has not travelled to the United Kingdom directly from the country in which he or she fears persecution, but via one or more "safe" countries, then the application may be summarily refused, ie without substantive consideration of the merits of the asylum claim, on the grounds that the applicant can be returned to a "safe third country".[5]

Under the new procedures established by the Asylum and Immigration Appeals Act 1993, all unsuccessful applicants (including those refused on "safe third country" grounds) have a right of appeal to the Immigration Appeals Authority (IAA). Appeals must normally be lodged within 10 working days of the refusal, and are heard by a single Special Adjudicator (who must hear and determine the appeal within 42 days of it being lodged). If the appeal is dismissed by the Special Adjudicator there is a further right of appeal, subject to leave and on a point of law only, to a three-member Immigration Appeals Tribunal (IAT).[6]

However, in those cases where the application has been refused on "safe third country" grounds, or on the grounds that the application is "frivolous or vexatious", the appeal must be lodged within 48 hours of the refusal if the applicant is held in detention (or within 10 working days if the applicant has been granted temporary admission and the notice of refusal is posted to the applicant, rather than being served in person), the Special Adjudicator must hear and determine the appeal within seven working days of it being lodged, and there is no further right of appeal to the IAT. In such cases the only further remedy

---

[5] This is the so-called "safe third country" rule, set out in Paragraph 345 of the Immigration Rules. A refusal on "safe third country" grounds can be made very quickly, within hours of the application being made. In 1994, 5.2% of all refusals were made on "safe third country" grounds. For further information on Amnesty International's concerns relating to such practice, see *United Kingdom: Passing the buck – deficient Home Office practice in "safe third country" asylum cases*, (July 1993)

[6] In the event that a further appeal to the IAT is made and dismissed, there is also a further right of appeal, subject to leave and on a point of law only, to the Court of Appeal. However, this provision is rarely used, with most appeals on a point of law being fully dealt with at the IAT stage

available once the appeal has been dismissed by a Special Adjudicator is the seeking of judicial review in the High Court.

All unsuccessful appellants are then liable to removal (ie, expulsion), either to their country of origin or, in "safe third country" cases, to the last "safe" country through which they travelled before reaching the United Kingdom.

The legal basis for detention

As described above, the *initial* examination of the asylum-seeker in "port" cases and "illegal entrant" cases is carried out by an Immigration Officer, who then passes the results of this examination to the Home Office Asylum Division for determination. Unlike the officials in the Asylum Division, Immigration Officers are general immigration functionaries who receive minimal training in asylum issues and, in general, have no specialist knowledge of the political and human rights situation in refugee-producing countries.

In all such cases, the Immigration Officer is empowered to detain the applicant pending determination of the asylum claim by the Asylum Division. In "port" cases, this power to detain is derived from Paragraph 16(1) of Schedule 2 to the Immigration Act 1971, while in "illegal entrant" cases it is derived from Paragraph 16(2) of Schedule 2.[7] The Act does not specify any limit on the length of such detention.

However, in all such cases the Immigration Officer has a discretionary power to temporarily admit the applicant rather than detain him or her. Paragraph 21(1) of Schedule 2 states that "a person liable to detention or detained under paragraph 16 above may, under the written

---

[7] These powers of detention are general powers that may be applied, not only to asylum-seekers, but to any person seeking leave to enter or remain in the UK and who, under the provisions of the 1971 Immigration Act, is subject to immigration control. In 1994, over 10,000 persons – of whom only a minority were seeking asylum – were detained overnight or longer under these powers. At any one time, some 200-300 persons not seeking asylum are held under these powers.

authority of an immigration officer, be temporarily admitted to the United Kingdom ... but this shall not prejudice a later exercise of the power to detain him" (ie, those granted temporary admission remain liable to detention). The decision on whether to detain or grant temporary admission (TA) is taken by the Immigration Officer (and confirmed by a Chief Immigration Officer) once he or she has completed the initial examination of the applicant, and the granting of TA is normally subject to conditions such as residing at a fixed address and reporting regularly to a local police station or immigration office.

Although detailed figures are not available, it is clear that TA is granted in the majority of such cases. For example, during the 18-month period July 1993 to December 1994, there were over 14,300 "port" asylum cases alone, and yet the greatest recorded number of "port" case asylum-seekers in detention at any one time was 360 (on 17 February 1994). In 1993, "about 25%" of the 2,275 asylum-seekers treated as "illegal entrants" during the year were detained "at some stage".[8] The limited statistical information available suggests that, in 1994, somewhere between 5% and 10% of all asylum applicants were detained for any length of time. The Home Office has stated that:

"... it is our policy to use detention only as a last resort. Temporary admission is granted wherever possible and detention is authorised only where there are good grounds for believing that the person will not comply with the terms of temporary admission. In deciding whether to detain account is taken of all relevant circumstances, including the means by which the person arrived in this country, any relevant immigration history, and any existing connections with the United Kingdom. In practice only a very small proportion of asylum-seekers is detained".[9]

---

[8] Source: letter to Ms Barbara Roche, MP, dated 12 December 1994, from Home Office minister Mr Nicholas Baker, MP

[9] Letter to Amnesty International, dated 14 April 1994, from Home Office minister Mr Charles Wardle, MP

Of the 572 asylum-seekers held in detention on 13 January 1995, 305 (53%) were "port" cases, and 210 (37%) were "illegal entrant" cases.[10]

In "deportation" cases the Immigration Officer may authorise detention (or continued detention, as the applicant is often already detained in such cases) under Paragraph 2 of Schedule 3 to the 1971 Immigration Act. Although there is no specific legal provision for the granting of TA in such cases, Immigration Officers can (and do) exercise discretion when deciding whether to authorise detention. Fifty-seven of the 572 asylum-seekers held in detention on 13 January 1995 were "deportation" cases.

The Asylum and Immigration Appeals Act 1993 effectively extended these powers of detention to those asylum cases where, at the time of application, the applicant has permission to be in the United Kingdom on another basis. Section 7 of the Act provides that, once the asylum claim of such an applicant has been refused by the Home Office, their original permission to be in the country may be curtailed and they may be detained (under Immigration Act powers) pending removal. Between July 1993 and early 1995, Section 7's provisions were rarely used, in line with guarantees given by ministers, prior to the Act coming into force, that these provisions would be used exceptionally. However, on 15 February 1995, the Home Office announced its intention to make "wider use" of the curtailment powers set out in Section 7.[11] It remains to be seen whether this will lead to the widespread use of detention in such cases.

International standards and the detention of asylum-seekers

International standards for the treatment of refugees make clear that

---

[10] Parliamentary Debates (Hansard), 18 January 1995, col 531-533, (written answer)
[11] Home Office News Release 037/95, 15 February 1995

asylum-seekers should not normally be held in detention, and set out clear criteria governing the particular circumstances in which such detention may be resorted to. In particular, Conclusion 44 of the intergovernmental Executive Committee of the Programme of the United Nations High Commissioner for Refugees (UNHCR) states that:

> *"... in view of the hardship which it involves, detention should normally be avoided. If necessary, detention should be resorted to only on grounds prescribed by law to verify identity; to determine the elements on which the claim to refugee status or asylum is based; to deal with cases where refugees or asylum-seekers have destroyed their travel documents in order to mislead the authorities of the State in which they intend to claim asylum; or to protect national security or public order".*[12]

The notion of "necessity" contained in UNHCR ExCom Conclusion 44 is of crucial significance, since it places the onus on the detaining authorities to demonstrate why other measures short of detention are not sufficient. Moreover, even if an asylum-seeker is detained for one of the grounds recognised as legitimate in Conclusion 44, detention should not continue longer than is strictly necessary. For example, detention "to verify identity" or "to determine the elements on which the claim to ... asylum is based" is permitted only for a *limited* period of such length as is reasonably necessary for the purpose. In most cases, this should not be more than one or two days.

In addition to the grounds set out in UNHCR ExCom Conclusion 44, it is generally recognised that detention may be resorted to in those

---

[12] UNHCR ExCom Conclusion 44 ('Detention of Refugees and Asylum-seekers'), adopted by consensus in 1986 by the governments then participating in the Executive Committee of UNHCR (including the UK). Since 1975 the Executive Committee has adopted a number of *Conclusions on the International Protection of Refugees*, setting out a number of basic requirements which States' asylum procedures should satisfy. Under Article 35 of the 1951 UN Convention, contracting states 'undertake to cooperate' with UNHCR and 'shall in particular facilitate its duty of supervising the application of the Convention'. It seems reasonable to conclude that such cooperation should include compliance with these UNHCR ExCom Conclusions.

cases where the asylum-seeker is likely to abscond if granted some form of temporary admission to the country. As noted above, the Government has cited this as the principal ground for its use of detention. However, it is also recognised that this ground for detention must be interpreted strictly: there must be *clear and convincing* evidence that the particular individual in question is likely to abscond.[13] Many governments abuse this ground for detention by applying it too widely to groups of asylum-seekers or to individuals for whom there is no *specific* evidence that they are likely to abscond.

As well as prescribing the circumstances in which detention of asylum-seekers may be resorted to, UNHCR ExCom Conclusion 44 also makes clear that all decisions to detain an asylum-seeker must be subject to due process:

> *"... detention measures taken in respect of refugees and asylum seekers should be subject to judicial or administrative review".*

Similarly, Article 9(4) of the International Covenant on Civil and Political Rights (ICCPR), to which the United Kingdom is a State Party and with which it is therefore bound to comply, provides that "Anyone who is deprived of his liberty by arrest or detention shall be entitled to take proceedings before a court, in order that court may decide without delay on the lawfulness of his detention and order his release if the detention is not lawful." Article 5(4) of the 1950 European Convention on Human Rights (ECHR), to which the United Kingdom is also a State Party, contains similar guarantees.

The United Nations *Body of Principles for the Protection of All Persons under Any Form of Detention or Imprisonment*, adopted by the UN

---

[13] Although the likelihood of absconding is not explicitly included in Conclusion 44, recognised experts on international refugee law have indicated that if (and only if) there is adequate and specific evidence that an individual is likely to abscond, then this would be recognised as a legitimate ground for detention.

General Assembly in 1988, also stresses the importance of independent scrutiny of the position of a detainee. Principle 4 states that "Any form of detention or imprisonment and all measures affecting the human rights of a person under any form of detention or imprisonment shall be ordered by, or be subject to the effective control of, a judicial or other authority", while Principle 11 states that "A person shall not be kept in detention without being given an effective opportunity to be heard promptly by a judicial or other authority". The term "judicial or other authority" is defined at the outset of the Body of Principles as "a judicial or other authority under the law whose status and tenure shall afford the strongest possible guarantees of competence, impartiality, and independence".

Inter alia, the UN Body of Principles provides: a) that the detainee must be given "prompt and full communication" of the reasons for detention (Principle 11), together with "information on and an explanation of" his or her rights and how to exercise them (Principle 13); b) that the detainee should have prompt, adequate, and regular access to legal representation (Principle 18); c) that there should be a prompt and *automatic* review of the reasons for detention by an independent authority (Principle 11); and d) that, in addition to this initial, automatic hearing to review the basis of detention, the detainee should subsequently be able to challenge the reasons for detention before an independent authority at any time on his or her initiative (Principle 32).

UNHCR ExCom Conclusion 44 also states that:

"... the conditions of detention of refugees and asylum-seekers must be humane. In particular, refugees and asylum-seekers shall, whenever possible, not be accommodated with persons detained as common criminals."

THE STUDY: SOME BASIC FINDINGS AND GENERAL REMARKS

Outcome of the asylum application

As of 31 March 1995, 37 of the 50 cases in this study have been fully resolved. Four of the detainees (one each from Lebanon, Algeria, Iran and Turkey) were released from detention and granted asylum by the Home Office (Cases 7, 23, 31 and 47). Three of the detainees (one each from Zaire, Congo and Turkey) were eventually granted asylum after their appeal to the Immigration Appeals Authority (IAA) was allowed (Cases 24, 42 and 45). One detainee (from Somalia) was eventually granted Exceptional Leave to Remain (Case 49). Six detainees withdrew their asylum applications and made voluntary departures from the United Kingdom, and 23 were expelled after being refused asylum and having their appeals to the IAA dismissed (see also Appendix 1). Amnesty International has investigated, but to date has not been able to substantiate, reports that one of those expelled was arrested and imprisoned upon his return to Angola (Case 12).

Of the 13 as yet unresolved cases, two of the applicants are still awaiting an initial decision on their asylum claim by the Home Office; six have been refused asylum but are awaiting the outcome of their appeal to the IAA; one has been refused asylum but is awaiting the outcome of a reconsideration of his case by the Home Office; and four, having been refused asylum and having had their appeals to the IAA dismissed, are awaiting removal. Of these 13 applicants, one has been released on bail by the Immigration Appeals Tribunal (IAT), and the others have been released on temporary admission (TA) by the Immigration Service. One of those awaiting removal is known to have absconded (see below).

Two aspects of these results are worthy of comment. Firstly, four of the detainees in this study (8%) were eventually recognised as refugees and granted asylum by the Home Office, compared with 4.2% of asylum applicants generally in the 18-month period July 1993 to December 1994. A further three detainees (6%) were recognised as refugees and granted asylum after having their appeal to the IAA allowed. This finding strongly suggests that the proportion of 'strong' asylum claims among those in detention is as great as, if not actually greater than, that among asylum applicants generally, and undermines ministers' and officials' attempts to imply that the asylum claims of those in detention are inherently weaker than those, the overwhelming majority, who are granted TA while their applications are considered.[14]

Secondly, six of the detainees (12%) withdrew their asylum application and made a voluntary departure from the UK, having spent an an average of 130 days in detention (Cases 9, 16, 32, 34, 41 and 43). This is a considerably larger proportion than that among asylum applicants generally (3% in 1993, the latest year for which figures are available[15]), and heightens Amnesty International's long-standing concern that the debilitating effects of prolonged detention may cause some detainees to abandon their asylum application before it is fully resolved, with an attendant risk that some may return to the country from which they have fled and where they may face persecution. Although in each of these six cases the detainee had been refused asylum, in four cases the detainee's appeal to the IAA had yet to be heard at the time he withdrew his application, and in a fifth case the appeal had not yet been fully dealt with.

---

[14] Ministers' and officials' letters and statements about the detention of asylum-seekers invariably begin with statements such as 'the great majority of those seeking asylum in the United Kingdom are not refugees' and 'the great majority [of detainees] have had their [asylum] applications refused' (letter to Amnesty International, dated 14 April 1994, from Home Office minister Mr Charles Wardle, MP).

[15] Source: letter to Ms Barbara Roche, MP, dated 12 December 1994, from Home Office minister Mr Nicholas Baker, MP

Duration of detention

Total time spent in detention before release (on TA or bail) or expulsion ranged from 32 days to 506 days (see also Appendix 1), while the average duration of detention was 158 days (just over five months). In 15 cases (30%) the detainee was held for more than six months, and in two of these cases the detainee was held for more than 12 months. Table 1 below gives a breakdown by duration of detention.

Table 1: Duration of detention

Time in detention	Number of cases
Less than 2 months	5
2 to 4 months	17
4 to 6 months	13
6 to 8 months	8
8 to 10 months	4
Over 10 months	3

The seven detainees ultimately granted asylum spent an average of 132 days in detention before being released; one man was held for 297 days (almost 10 months), and another for 145 days. The six female detainees spent an average of 125 days in detention; one woman was held for 294 days (almost 10 months) and another for 146 days.

These findings contradict the Government's claim that the new asylum procedures introduced under the Asylum and Immigration Appeals Act 1993 would lead to "shorter periods of detention on average".[16] Indeed, the results of this study strongly suggest that the average duration of detention has actually *increased* significantly since July 1993. Although the Home Office does not publish any figures on which the average duration of detention among all detainees could be calculated, the proportion of detainees in this study who spent four months or more in detention (56%) represents a considerable increase

---

[16] Letter to a member of Amnesty International, dated 26 October 1993, from Immigration Service HQ

on the 34% held for the same length of time among the 230 asylum-seekers in detention on 3 April 1993, shortly before the Act came into force.[17] The Home Office itself has also conceded an increase in the average duration of detention, stating that "the appeals process introduced with the 1993 Asylum and Immigration Appeals Act has added to the time asylum applicants now spend in detention".[18]

The average duration of detention experienced by the 50 asylum-seekers in this study, 158 days, is also considerably longer than that experienced by criminal remand prisoners (eg those awaiting trial at a Magistrates Court or Crown Court). In the 12-month period ending May 1994 such remand prisoners spent an average of 56 days in prison before being released or convicted.[19] In other words, on average the asylum-seekers in this study, none of whom had been charged with any criminal offence, were incarcerated for almost three times as long as remand prisoners charged with serious criminal offences.

The finding that almost one-third of the detainees in this study were held for more than six months mirrors the current situation among detainees in general. Of the 619 asylum-seekers held in detention on 29 March 1995, for example, 190 (30.7%) had been in detention longer than six months (see also Appendix 2).

Release from detention
Four of the detainees (Cases 6, 24, 36 and 42) were released on bail by the IAA, after 294, 118, 35 and 106 days in detention respectively. A further 19 detainees were eventually released on TA by the Immigration Service, after an average of 140 days in detention. In six of these 23 cases the detainee was held for more than six months before being released on bail or TA. As of 31 March 1995, only one of those so

---

[17] Source: *Home Office Statistical Bulletin 19/93*

[18] Commentary in section on detention in *Home Office Stastical Bulletin 17/94*. (July 1994)

[19] Parliamentary Debates (Hansard), 19 July 1994, col 173, (written answer)

released on bail or TA is known to have absconded or otherwise failed to comply with any conditions attached to his or her release: in Case 10, the applicant was granted TA shortly after his appeal to the IAA was dismissed, but he subsequently failed to attend for removal.

These findings seriously undermine the Government's claim that detention is used only where necessary and "only as a last resort" when the "applicant cannot be relied upon to comply voluntarily with the terms of TA". The fact that so many of the detainees (46%) could be released on bail or TA after lengthy periods of detention ($4^1/_2$ months, on average), with only one of them subsequently absconding, begs the question of why the 22 individuals who did not abscond were detained in the first place. In each case the alternative accommodation (provided by friends, relatives or a refugee agency or community group) to which the detainee was eventually allowed to go was available long before his or her release.

Immigration Officers make decisions to detain without reference or effective accountability to any court or independent review body. There is no requirement for the detainee to be taken before a court within a fixed time period, or indeed at any time. There is therefore no automatic opportunity for the detainee to challenge the basis of the decision to detain (of which he or she is not adequately informed in any case), and therefore no means by which the detainee can demonstrate that the decision to detain is mistaken, if indeed the reasons for detention are fallacious. The eventual release of 23 of the 50 detainees in this study, with only one of them subsequently absconding, strongly suggests to Amnesty International that the original decisions to detain in 22 of these 23 cases were indeed mistaken - ie, there were no real grounds for detention in the first place - and that the incarceration of these 22 individuals (44%), for an average of $4^1/_2$ months, was unnecessary.

Despite numerous requests from Amnesty International and other organisations over a period of several years, Home Office ministers and officials have repeatedly failed to provide any statistics that would substantiate their claim that the number of asylum-seekers who abscond after being granted temporary admission is a "significant problem" justifying current detention policy. In response to a number of written questions tabled by Members of Parliament in November and December 1994, for example, the Home Office minister, Nicholas Baker, declined to state how many cases involving asylum-seekers absconding have been recorded by the Home Office, stating simply that such information "is not available" or "is not recorded centrally".[20] In October 1994, however, when pressed on this issue during an interview for a BBC radio documentary about detention, Mr Baker conceded that the number of asylum-seekers who abscond each year is "small"[21]. And in February 1995, in response to further requests for statistics on absconders, Mr Baker produced figures showing that, of the 37,120 "persons who applied for asylum in-country and [were] refused asylum or exceptional leave [to remain]" in the three-year period 1992-94, only 220 (ie, 0.59%) "are known to have absconded or are classified as missing".[22] These figures support Amnesty International's belief that the "problem" of asylum-seekers absconding is nowhere near as significant as ministers and officials have previously claimed.

---

[20] Parliamentary Debates (Hansard), 3 November 1994, col 1338; 23 November 1994, col 159; and 8 December 1994 col 336 (written answers)

[21] *File on Four*, broadcast on BBC Radio 4 on 18 October 1994

[22] Parliamentary Debates (Hansard), 3 February 1995, col 896-899; and 16 February 1995, col 755-756 (written answers)

PROVIDING REASONS FOR DETENTION

Providing reasons: at the time of detention

It has long been apparent that the most basic flaw in existing detention practice is the absence of a mechanism by which detainees can be informed of the specific reasons for their detention. Not only is this a major cause of frustration and resentment among detainees (leading directly to friction between detainees and prison/detention centre staff and to protests such as the mass demonstration by detainees in Campsfield House in June 1994[23]), but it is a significant impediment to any legal challenge to the decision to detain. In defence of this omission, the Government has previously stated that "the reasons for detention are explained to the individual in a language he understands at the time of initial detention"[24]. Prior to October 1994, however, the various Immigration Service *Instructions to Staff on Detention* made no reference at all to the need to inform detainees of the reasons for their detention, either orally or in writing.[25] In practice, detainees have either been given no explanation of the decision to detain at all, or they have received bland, verbal explanations such as "I am detaining you because I am not satisfied that you will comply with the terms of temporary admission". Clearly, such explanations, whether verbal or in writing, are not sufficient: a detailed, written statement of the specific and *individualised* reasons for detention is essential if the detainee is to be able to mount an effective challenge to those reasons at some later stage, possibly many weeks after the time of initial detention.

---

[23] During an Amnesty International visit to HMP Rochester in November 1994, senior prison officers cited the Immigration Service's failure to adequately inform Immigration Act detainees of the specific reasons for their detention as the principle cause of friction between detainees and prison staff.
[24] Letter to the Refugee Legal Group, dated 18 April 1994, from Home Office minister Mr Charles Wardle, MP
[25] *Immigration Service Instructions to Staff on Detention*, dated 3 December 1991 and 20 September 1994

In this study, none of the 50 detainees was given, at the time of being detained, a written statement of the reasons for detention, and indeed there is clearly no mechanism for providing an asylum-seeker who is to be detained with such a statement. This is a violation of international standards, which require the authorities to provide "prompt and full communication" of the reasons for detention in each case.[26]

Providing reasons: at any stage

In 47 cases the detainee was not, at any stage, given a written statement of the reasons for detention. However, in three cases (Cases 10, 24 and 50), a written statement of the reasons for detention was eventually provided. In all three cases the detainee had applied to the Immigration Appeals Authority (IAA) for bail, and the statement, headed 'Bail Summary' and prepared by the Immigration Service, was given to the detainee's legal representative by the Home Office representative at the bail hearing.

In each case the Bail Summary sets out the Immigration Service's reasons for opposing the granting of bail, and constitutes a reasonably full explanation of the reasons for detention in the first place. However, by the time the Bail Summary was made available (at the bail hearing) the three detainees had spent 110 days, 118 days and 74 days in detention respectively. Such a delay in the provision of this information does not satisfy the requirement, under international standards, for the detainee to be given "prompt" communication of the reasons for detention.

Moreover, there is clearly no obligation on the Home Office to give a Bail Summary to the detainee's legal representative at the bail hearing (or indeed at any other stage). It was apparent that a Bail Summary was

---

[26] ECHR Article 5(2), ICCPR Article 9(2), and UN Body of Principles (Principle 11 and 32). Principle 11(2) makes clear that the detainee and his or her legal representative, if any, "shall receive prompt and full communication of any order of detention, together with the reasons therefor".

prepared by the Immigration Service (for the benefit of the Home Office representative) in all 17 cases where there was a bail hearing, yet in 14 of these cases it was not made available to the detainee or his/her legal representative. Several legal representatives confirmed to Amnesty International that they were not aware of the existence of such Bail Summaries (and had therefore not requested one), while in one case (Case 42) the legal representative's request to be given the Bail Summary was refused by the Home Office representative. Indeed, it would appear that the provision of the Bail Summary in Cases 10, 24 and 50 was inadvertent.

The principal significance of the provision of the Bail Summary in these three cases is that it begs the question of why such a written statement cannot be provided, at a much earlier stage, in *all* cases. Given that a mechanism for the production of such written explanations of the decision to detain by the Immigration Service already exists, it would appear to be a relatively straightforward step for the Home Office to make provision of this statement to the detainee, at the time of detention or promptly thereafter, a routine matter, thereby bringing this area of detention practice into line with international standards.

Providing information on the detainee's rights while in detention
None of the 50 detainees was given, either at the time of detention or at any later stage, a full, written explanation of his or her rights in detention and how to exercise them, and again it is clear that there is no mechanism for providing detainees with such information. For example, the detainees were not informed of their right to seek bail, or how to go about making an application for bail to the IAA or the courts. Similarly, although posters giving the address and telephone numbers of the Refugee Legal Centre, an organisation providing free legal advice and assistance to asylum-seekers, are prominently displayed in the three Immigration Service detention centres, these posters were not on

display in any of the criminal prisons holding asylum-seekers visited by Amnesty International during the course of this study (including HMP Rochester). Many of the detainees held in criminal prisons appeared to rely on Probation Officers to assist them with obtaining information on how to contact refugee support agencies. This is a violation of international standards, which require that all detainees be fully informed of their rights while in detention and how to avail themselves of such rights.[27]

Reasons for detention: some general remarks

The lack of any detailed statement of the specific reasons for detention in all but three cases precludes any meaningful analysis of the validity of the decisions to detain the 50 asylum-seekers in this study. However, in 34 of the 45 cases where an application for TA was made to the Immigration Service by the detainee's legal representative (either by telephone or in writing), Immigration Officers offered a variety of limited 'explanations' of the decision to detain (in general, such 'explanations' of the decision to detain were given orally, rather than in writing).

In six of these 34 cases, the 'explanations' given were so bland as to be meaningless, eg "the applicant is not considered suitable for TA" and "the applicant is unlikely to comply with the terms of TA". In one case, where the detainee's legal representative pressed the Immigration Officer to expand on his earlier (verbal) statement that the individual "is not a suitable candidate for TA", the Immigration Officer refused, stating: "I do not have to give reasons" (Case 14). In another case, where the cover-sheet of the Immigration Service's internal file was inadvertently passed to the detainee's legal representative, the entry headed 'Reasons for Detention' stated simply: "Refused leave to enter.

---

[27] UN Body of Principles (Principle 13) provides that detainees shall be given 'information on and an explanation of' their rights and how to avail themselves of such rights "at the moment of arrest and at the commencement of detention or imprisonment, or promptly thereafter"

Detained pending removal" (Case 26).

But the two most commonly cited 'reasons' for detention were that "the applicant arrived without documents" or "with forged documents" (cited in 18 cases) and "the applicant has no relatives in the UK" (cited in seven cases).[28] The applicant's lack of valid documents on arrival and immediate lack of "prospective hosts" were also cited as the principal "factors in the decision to detain" in two of the three Immigration Service Bail Summaries made available (see above). Not only are such reasons non-specific, ie they could be applied to most asylum-seekers, but, as grounds for detention, they are inconsistent with international standards, which do not permit the detention of asylum-seekers simply because they have arrived without valid documents.

In Case 8, for example, Amnesty International wrote to the Home Office to express its concern regarding the detention of Mr K, and to seek clarification of the reasons for his detention. At that time, Mr K had been held in detention for over three months and, even though a local family was now offering to accommodate him, an application for TA by his legal representative had recently been refused, without adequate explanation. In reply, a senior Immigration Service official stated that Mr K had been detained "because he had no documents on arrival and because no suitable sponsors were available", and that "the need for continued detention has been reviewed regularly and we are satisfied that this remains justified". [29] A mere four days after the date of this reply, however, Mr K was released on TA by the Immigration Service (after 101 days in detention), on the sole condition that he reside at the local family's address. In subsequent correspondence, the Immigration Service has failed to clarify the reasons for this sudden (and

---

[28] In five cases, both these 'reasons' were cited. Other 'reasons' for detention cited by Immigration Officers included the fact that the application applied for asylum only after his of her existing permission to be in the UK had expired (two cases) , and the Immigration Service's assement of the individual as a "suicide risk" (two cases)

[29] Letter to Amnesty International, dated 28 March 1994, from the Deputy Director (Enforcement), Immigration Service HQ

unexplained) change in its position but, given that suitable sponsors *were* available on the date of the official's reply to Amnesty International, it would appear that the sole reason for the Immigration Service's conclusion that Mr K's detention remained "justified" was his arrival "without documents".

It must be borne in mind that the majority of those applying for asylum in the United Kingdom each year arrive without documents or with fraudulent documents. [30] As the Executive Committee of UNHCR has noted, "circumstances may compel a refugee or asylum-seeker to have recourse to fraudulent documentation when leaving a country in which his physical safety or freedom are threatened". [31] In some cases this is because they are unable to obtain valid travel documents from their own authorities. In other cases it is because the use of a false identity (and therefore fraudulent documentation) is necessary to evade controls on departure: the Turkish border police, for example, check the names of all those leaving Turkey against computer records of wanted political suspects.

But, in most cases, it is because the use of fraudulent documents (or clandestine methods of travel) is the only means of by-passing the visa regimes that have been imposed in recent years on nationals of all major refugee-producing countries. As the Home Office itself has noted, "the Immigration Rules make no provision for a visa to be granted to enable someone to come to the UK as a refugee" and any person applying for a visa at a British Embassy or High Commission who reveals, or is suspected of having, an intention of seeking asylum in the United Kingdom is almost certain to have their visa application refused. Since March 1987 the Government has also, under the Immigration (Carri-

---

[30] Of the 6,725 applications for asylum made at Heathrow, Gatwick and Dover in 1993, for example, "an estimated 40% were without travel documents and 20% were in possession of fraudulent travel documents", Parliamentary Debates (Hansard), 3 November 1994, col 1338, Mr Nicholas Baker, MP (written answer)
[31] UNHCR ExCom Conclusion 58

ers' Liability) Act 1987, imposed a financial penalty (currently £2,000 per passenger) on any airline or shipping company bringing passengers lacking a valid visa where one is required, with the aim of inducing such companies to check, prior to embarkation, that all would-be passengers hold a valid visa.

The most obvious means of by-passing such measures is to obtain fraudulent documentation, which is now freely available - often at a considerable price - from profiteers. These profiteers frequently travel with the purchaser and reclaim the documentation immediately before arrival (presumably for re-use), or advise the purchaser to destroy the documentation *en route* (presumably to destroy all evidence of the documentation's source). The only other means of by-passing these measures is to travel without valid documents and attempt to enter the country clandestinely (eg in the back of a lorry): again, unscrupulous profiteers will arrange such travel - at a price.

Many asylum-seekers also have no friends or relatives in the United Kingdom to offer accommodation, but temporary accommodation can invariably be obtained through refugee agencies or community groups. Such accommodation was available to, if not actually used by, at least 45 of the detainees in this study.

And yet, as the Government itself has repeatedly emphasised, the 600 or so asylum-seekers held in detention represent less than 1.5% of the 56,000 cases currently under consideration. In other words, the Home Office is able to deal with over 98.5% of asylum cases *without* resorting to the use of detention and, apparently, without any significant problem of asylum-seekers absconding, despite the fact that in the great majority of these cases the asylum-seeker will have arrived without documents (or with fraudulent documents) and/or has no friends or relatives in the United Kingdom, the 'reasons' for detention most commonly cited by Immigration Officers.

Moreover, international standards do not permit asylum-seekers to be detained simply because they have used fraudulent identity documents or have destroyed their documents. As noted above, UNHCR ExCom Conclusion 58 makes clear that "circumstances may compel a refugee or asylum-seeker to have recourse to fraudulent documentation". The 1951 UN Convention on Refugees also implicitly recognises that asylum-seekers may need to use fraudulent documentation to escape persecution, and provides (in Article 31) that "States shall not impose penalties" on refugees "on account of their illegal entry or presence". Under the terms of UNHCR ExCom Conclusion 44, asylum-seekers may be detained on such grounds *only* if the authorities can demonstrate that they have used fraudulent documents or destroyed their documents *"with the intention to mislead the authorities"* of the state in which they intend to claim asylum. In the light of Article 31 of the Convention and UNHCR ExCom Conclusion 58, an asylum-seeker who uses fraudulent documents or destroys documents simply in order to gain entry to the asylum procedure has not necessarily shown such an intention. The essential point is whether *after* gaining access to the asylum procedure the asylum-seeker persists in trying to mislead the authorities about his or her identity.

This vacuity of the 'explanation' of the decision to detain in so many of the cases in this study heightens Amnesty International's long-standing concern that, in many cases, the decision to detain appears to be an arbitrary one, dependent less upon a subjective and considered assessment of whether detention is actually necessary, than on the availability of detention places on any given day and more nebulous factors such as the individual Immigration Officer's demeanour and disposition towards asylum-seekers. Invariably, it is not possible to discern any substantive reason for the detention of the individual in question and Immigration Officers, when pressed to explain the decision to detain, resort to bland and formulaic justifications.

Reasons for detention: the Government's response

In its formal response to the original edition of this report, the Government expressed agreement that "detainees should be fully informed of [the] reasons for detention", but stated that "this is best done *orally* ... if a written statement were to be provided as a matter of routine it would only be effective if it were translated into a language fully understood by the detainee, which would be time-consuming and cause delays". [32] At the same time, the Immigration Service issued a new *Instruction to Staff on Detention*, stating that:

> "It is essential that all staff ensure that when a person is to be detained the reasons for detention are explained to the individual fully, in a language he or she understands. It is not sufficient to state merely that the Immigration Service is not satisfied that the person will comply with the terms of temporary admission. The reasons for making the decision to detain must relate to the individual factors of the case and be explained as fully as possible.

> Once the individual has been notified of the reasons for detention this should be recorded on the detention record (Form IS93). When the review of detention is carried out by an Inspector, within 24 hours of the original decision, he/she should ensure that the reasons have indeed been recorded, and adequately justify the decision."

Amnesty International very much welcomes the Government's recognition, signified by the issuing of this new instruction to Immigration Service staff, that immigration officials have previously failed to provide detainees and their legal representatives with adequate expla-

[32] Letter to Amnesty International, dated 15 November 1994, from Home Office minister Mr Nicholas Baker, MP

nations of the reasons for detention. As noted above, all previous *Instructions to Staff on Detention* lacked any reference to the need to inform detainees of the reasons for detention. The organisation hopes very much that this new instruction will in future result in all detainees being given full oral explanations of the *specific* and *individualised* reasons for their detention, as well as in those reasons being recorded in detail on the internal Immigration Service file (ie, Form IS93).

However, the organisation believes that, now that the specific and individualised reasons for detention are to be recorded, in writing, on Form IS93, there is absolutely no reason why these could not be provided, *in writing*, to the detainee and his or her legal representative. The organisation simply cannot accept the Government's argument that it is preferable for detainees to be informed *orally* of the individualised reasons for detention, rather than in writing. Nor can it accept that a written statement "would only be effective if it were translated into a language fully understood by the detainee". While it is clearly *ideal* that detainees are fully informed of the reasons for detention in a language that they fully understand, it would undoubtedly be a major step in the right direction for detainees to be informed, in writing, of the specific and individualised reasons for detention *in English*. Even if the detainee is not able to fully comprehend the content of such a written statement, his or her legal representative would be able to do so and, if appropriate, would then be able to seek to challenge those reasons before the courts or the IAA. It is difficult not to conclude that this is precisely what the Home Office hopes to avoid by not making the reasons available in writing.

Amnesty International also rejects the Government's argument that the financial costs associated with providing written statements of the reasons for detention would be prohibitive. Ministers and officials have failed to provide any figure for the likely costs of providing such statements, but Amnesty International is confident that the cost of providing the detainee and/or his or her legal representative with a transcription of the specific and individualised reasons for detention recorded on the Immigration Service file (in line with the new instruction to Immigration Service staff) is most unlikely to be excessive. As described above, the Immigration Service already has a mechanism for preparing such written statements in the minority of cases where a bail hearing takes place. At the very most, the Immigration Service would simply have to produce a new form, onto which Immigration Officers would simply transcribe what they have already recorded on Form IS93, and which would then be handed to the detainee and/or passed to the detainee's legal representative. Clearly, this would take no more than a few minutes of the Immigration Officer's time. Amnesty International has suggested that the total costs associated with taking such steps would be in the order of £10,000 per year, a relatively insignificant sum when set against the total costs of detention policy (possibly as much as £20 million per year). Despite being invited to do so, ministers have not provided any information or argument to rebut this estimate.

Intriguingly, since the original publication of this report the Home Office appears to have abandoned an earlier commitment - albeit one possibly given in error - to the giving of reasons for detention in writing. In September 1994, Mr Baker wrote to another Member of Parliament, stating that "the reasons for detention are explained orally to the individual ... and these will also be provided to him or his representatives in writing, if requested".[33] To Amnesty International's knowledge, the latter part of this sentence has not appeared in any subsequent correspondence from Mr Baker, and none of the *Instructions to Staff on Detention* include any reference to the need to provide the reasons for detention in writing when requested to do so by legal representatives. As noted above, Immigration Officers have displayed - and continue to

---

[33] Letter to Ms Bridget Prentice, MP, dated 14 September 1994, from Mr Nicholas Baker, MP (ref: PO 18139/94)

display - a marked reluctance to give any kind of written response to legal representatives' requests for an explanation of the decision to detain.

REVIEW OF DETENTION

Introduction

Prior to September 1994, the Government defended its detention of asylum-seekers by citing, *inter alia*, three separate mechanisms by which the initial decision to detain is or may be reviewed: i) internal Immigration Service reviews; ii) an application for bail to the courts; and iii) an application for bail to the Immigration Appeals Authority (IAA). Ministers and officials repeatedly claimed that "these provisions ... provide adequate checks and there is no justification for introducing a further review procedure".[34]

Since September 1994, however, ministers and officials have repeatedly stated that, in addition to the above mechanisms, "detention may also be challenged in the courts by way of an application for *habeas corpus*", and that these four mechanisms "provide proper safeguards".[35] Each of these mechanisms is examined in turn below.

Internal Immigration Service reviews

According to the Home Office, "all detention is reviewed locally at least every seven days. After one month, the case is reviewed at Immigration Service Headquarters monthly and at an increasingly senior level so that all those detained for six months or more are reviewed by a Director of the Immigration Service". However, not only is there clearly no *independent* element to these Immigration Service reviews, but the reviews are undertaken without any input from the detainee or his/her legal representative, and there is therefore no effective opportunity for the detainee to challenge the reasons for detention (of which he or she

---

[34] Letter to the Refugee Legal Group, dated 18 April 1994, from Home Office minister Mr Charles Wardle, MP
[35] Letter to Mr Christopher Gill, MP, dated 21 December 1994, from Home Office minister Mr Nicholas Baker, MP

is not, in any case, properly informed) or to provide new information.

Moreover, given the vacuity of so many of the 'reasons' for detention cited by Immigration Officers in response to enquiries from detainees' legal representatives, it is highly questionable whether these internal reviews amount to more than a 'rubber-stamping' of the original decision to detain. In Case 26, for example, where the coversheet of the Immigration Service's internal file (Form IS93) was inadvertently passed to the detainee's legal representative, the entry headed 'Reasons for Detention' stated simply "Refused leave to enter. Detained pending removal". This detainee was held for a total of 154 days (five months), which means that the original decision to detain should have been reviewed by a senior officer at Immigration Service Headquarters on at least four occasions. It is difficult to envisage how senior officers could have carried out an effective review of the original decision to detain on the basis of such meagre information.

Therefore, while it is highly desirable that some form of internal review of the original decision to detain be undertaken, this mechanism simply does not satisfy the requirement, under international standards, that all decisions to detain must be subject to "the effective control of a judicial or other authority",[36] and cannot be regarded as a satisfactory review mechanism.

Applications for bail to the courts
Technically, a detained asylum-seeker can apply to the High Court for bail. However, such an application for bail can only be made once the detainee has made an application to the High Court for judicial review of a Home Office or IAA decision on his or her asylum claim, and that application is before the court. And, as a measure of last resort, any

---

[36] UN Body of Principles (Principle 4). ECHR Article 5, and ICCPR Article 9 also require judicial control of decisions to detain.

application for judicial review is likely to be made at or towards the end of the asylum procedure (eg following dismissal of an appeal by a Special Adjudicator and refusal of leave to appeal to the Immigration Appeals Tribunal), by which time the detainee may have spent months in detention.[37] Furthermore, the High Court has previously set out its reluctance to interfere with Immigration Officers' discretionary power to detain other than in the most extreme circumstances, eg where there is clear evidence of malice on the part of the Immigration Officer in question.[38]

Accordingly, it is clear from their comments to Amnesty International that most legal representatives consider judicial review and applications for bail to the High Court to have no value as a means of challenging detention in asylum cases. The Home Office itself has conceded that, while it does not hold any accurate figures, the number of detained asylum-seekers released on bail by the High Court in recent years "is likely to be small".[39]

In this study only three of the detainees (Cases 6, 23 and 40) applied to the High Court for judicial review of decisions on their asylum claim by the Home Office or IAA, and these applications were first considered by the court after 128, 238 and 97 days of detention respectively. None of the detainees applied to the court for bail, principally because their legal representatives considered such action to be pointless.

---

[37] Judicial review is a mechanism by which the High Court can test the validity of a decision by a lower court or an administrative decision by a local authority or, as in asylum cases, a government department. However, judicial review provides a procedural review only: it focuses not on the merits of the decision in question, but rather on whether the law and prescribed procedures have been followed, and is therefore a measure of last resort only. Before July 1993, applications to the High Court for judicial review were common in asylum cases, but since the introduction of a universal right of appeal under the Asylum and Immigration Appeals Act 1993 the value of such applications, and therefore their frequency, has decreased.

[38] See, for example, *Gurinder Singh Dillon* (1987) Imm AR 222

[39] Letter to Amnesty International, dated 14 October 1993, from the Head of the Home Office Asylum Division

Applications for a writ of habeas corpus

Any person held in detention by the authorities can apply to the High Court for a writ of *habeas corpus*. Under the Habeas Corpus Act 1816, the court is obliged to examine the validity of the detaining authority's power to detain the individual seeking the writ, ie to decide whether the individual's detention is provided for by law. The most common contemporary use of this Act is challenging the detention in police custody (of persons arrested on suspicion of a criminal offence) when time limits imposed by the Police and Criminal Evidence Act 1984 have been breached.

In the case of a detained asylum-seeker, however, the value of the right to seek a writ of *habeas corpus* is negated by the fact that this mechanism provides a *jurisdictional* review only: while it may examine the legitimacy of the Immigration Officer's power to detain, the court is not empowered to examine the *merits* of the decision to detain the individual in question. In other words, the court is only able to decide whether or not the detention of the individual in question is within the law, and cannot decide whether or not the grounds for his or her detention are correct. And of course, by virtue of Schedule 2 to the Immigration Act 1971, the indefinite detention of an asylum-seeker at the discretion of an Immigration Officer *is* within the law. This means that, to obtain his or her release by means of a writ for *habeas corpus*, an individual would have to demonstrate to the High Court's satisfaction not only that his or her detention is unlawful, but that *all* detention under Immigration Act powers is unlawful. It is unrealistic to suppose that the Government would tolerate any such ruling and, in the (unlikely) event of such a ruling being upheld on appeal to the Court of Appeal and House of Lords, the Government could be expected to take steps to amend the law in such a way as to nullify its effect.

This point was illustrated recently when a High Court ruling to grant writs of *habeas corpus* to four detained asylum-seekers - to Amnesty International's knowledge, the first ever ruling of its kind - was swiftly overturned by the Court of Appeal. In granting the writs, in January 1995, the High Court ruled that asylum-seekers cannot be detained pending a decision on their claim by the Home Office because, under Section 6 of the Asylum & Immigration Appeals Act 1993, Immigration Officers have no power to remove them from the United Kingdom while their applications for asylum are under consideration and the powers of detention bestowed on Immigration Officers (under Schedule 2 to the Immigration Act 1971) are ancillary to their powers to order removal.[40] The ruling reportedly caused "consternation" in the Home Office,[41] and indeed government lawyers sought and obtained an expedited appeal hearing before the Court of Appeal later the same week. The Court of Appeal promptly overturned the ruling, stating that there is "no reason, which can be derived from the provisions of the 1993 Act as applied to those of the 1971 Act, to attribute to Parliament the intention to deprive [Immigration Officers] of [their] discretionary power to detain", and concluding that the High Court had "come to a wrong conclusion on this issue".[42]

Had the High Court's ruling not been rapidly overturned by the Court of Appeal, the Home Office would have had to release large numbers of asylum-seekers from detention, and would also have faced compensation claims (for false imprisonment) by former detainees possibly totalling millions of pounds. Ministers were reported to be ready to introduce emergency legislation to reverse the effects of the ruling, in the event of it being upheld by the Court of Appeal.

---

[40] *Regina v Immigration Officer, Ex parte Khan and others*, Queen's Bench Division(Mr Justice Dyson), 16 January 1995. Because all four detainees had been deemed to be "illegal entrants", the ruling applied only to those asylum-seekers detained as "illegal entrants" and awaiting an initial decision on their claim by the Home Office, but lawyers anticipated being able to use the ruling to argue for the release of other categories of detained asylum-seekers.
[41] *The Guardian*, 18 January 1995
[42] *Secretary of State for the Home Department and another v Khan and others*, Court of Appeal, 3 February 1995

In short, therefore, the right to seek a writ of *habeas corpus* has no real value as a means of challenging the detention of an asylum-seeker under Immigration Act powers. In this study, none of the 50 detainees applied for a writ of *habeas corpus*.

Applications for bail to the IAA

In practice, therefore, the only means of seeking an *independent* review of the decision to detain is to apply for bail to the Immigration Appeals Authority (IAA). Applications for bail are normally made in writing (but may also be made orally at an appeal hearing), and are determined at an oral hearing by a single Special Adjudicator (or by the Immigration Appeals Tribunal, if the application is made when the applicant has an appeal pending before the IAT, rather than the IAA). In this study, 19 of the 50 detainees made an application for bail to the IAA: in three cases the detainee was released on TA before the application was fully heard, in 12 cases bail was refused by a Special Adjudicator, and in four cases the detainee was granted bail (see Table 3 below for further details). The findings of this study highlight two principal shortcomings of this mechanism as a means of ensuring an independent review of the reasons for detention.

The IAA bail process: restricted eligibility for bail

The most obvious shortcoming is that the right to apply for bail to the IAA is not universally available. In "port" cases, the detainee may apply for bail to the IAA after seven days have elapsed,[43] but in "illegal entrant" and "deportation" cases the detainee cannot apply for bail to the IAA until he or she has been refused asylum by the Home Office and has lodged an appeal against that refusal to the IAA.[44] Clearly, this may mean the detainee spending a long time in detention *without* the right to apply for bail. In this study, the 13 detainees deemed to be illegal

---

[43] Paragraph 22 of Schedule 2 to the 1971 Immigration Act
[44] Paragraph 29 of Schedule 2, and Paragraph 3 of Schedule 3, to the 1971 Immigration Act

entrants, and the one detainee who applied for asylum while facing deportation on other grounds, spent an average of 63 days (two months) in detention before becoming eligible to apply for bail. In one case, the detainee spent 127 days (over four months) in detention before becoming eligible to apply for bail, while the three "illegal entrants" ultimately granted asylum [45](Cases 7, 23 and 45) spent an average of 48 days in detention before becoming eligible (see also Table 2 below).

Table 2: Eligibility for bail in illegal entrant/deportation cases

Case	Comments	Days in detention without eligibility for bail
1	No bail application (no sureties available)	32
3	Bail application made to IAA; heard after 77 days in detention; bail refused by Special Adjudicator.	57
4	No bail application (no sureties available)	78
7	No bail application (no sureties available)	34
10	Bail application made to IAA; heard after 110 days in detention; bail refused by Special Adjudicator.	52
18	Bail application made to IAA; heard after 173 days in detention; bail refused by Special Adjudicator.	127
20	No bail application (no sureties available)	77
23	No bail application (no sureties available)	56
30	No bail application (no sureties available)	43
32	No bail application (no sureties available)	37
43	Bail application made to IAA; heard after 98 days in detention; bail refused by Special Adjudicator.	78
45	Bail application made to IAA; heard after 80 days in detention; bail refused by Special Adjudicator.	54
46	Released on TA (after 34 days in detention) before becoming eligible to apply for bail.	34
48	Released on TA (after 113 days in detention) before becoming eligible to apply for bail.	113
	Average number of days in detention before becoming eligible to apply for bail:	63

---

[45] In each of these three cases the applicant was initially refused asylum, but was subsequently recognised as a refugee and granted asylum after a reconsideration of the case by the Home Office or a successful appeal to the IAA.

The opportunity to apply for bail to the IAA, in practice the only means of seeking an independent review of the decision to detain, is therefore not available to all detainees at all times. This is a violation of international standards, which require that a detainee should be able to initiate a challenge to the reasons for detention *"at any time"*.[46] It is also a deficiency that affects a large number of detained asylum-seekers generally: of the 572 asylum-seekers in detention on 13 January 1995, for example, 282 (47%) were either "illegal entrant" or "deportation" cases.

Furthermore, this study shows that, in "illegal entrant" and "deportation" cases, the detainee is caught in a double bind: unable to apply for bail until he or she has been refused asylum and has lodged an appeal to the IAA, he or she is then likely to find the refusal of asylum being cited by the Home Office as a ground for opposing bail. In each of the five "illegal entrant" or "deportation" cases where a bail hearing took place, the Home Office representative argued that, as the applicant's asylum claim had now been refused, he was even more unlikely to comply with the terms of bail. Significantly, none of the five was granted bail by the IAA.

The IAA bail process: lack of an automatic hearing to review detention
The second principal shortcoming of the IAA bail process as a review mechanism is that it does not provide an *automatic* hearing to review the reasons for detention. Whether or not a bail hearing takes place at all depends primarily upon whether the detainee can find at least two persons willing to act as sureties (ie, sponsors) by placing a substantial recognizance[47] with the IAA.

---

[46] ECHR Article 5(4), ICCPR Article 9(4), and UN Body of Principles (Principle 32). Principle 32 provides that 'A detained person or his counsel shall be entitled at any time to take proceedings according to domestic law before a judicial or other authority to challenge the lawfulness of his detention in order to obtain his release without delay, if it is unlawful'.

[47] A sum of money that will normally be forfeited if the applicant, having been granted bail, subsequently absconds.

Although the relevant legislation[48] does not specify any minimum level of recognizance, it has in recent years become the norm for Special Adjudicators (and the IAT) to require total recognizances of several thousand pounds before granting bail. Guidelines issued to Adjudicators by the IAA in 1991 state that the amount of recognizance to be required is at their "discretion", but "rarely will an Adjudicator release an applicant on less than two sureties each in the sum of £1,000 recognizances and frequently recognizances will total £5,000".[49] Since 1991, these sums appear to have been revised upwards. This was confirmed in Case 37 of this study, where the Special Adjudicator, in refusing bail, stated that "there is a convention prevalent among my colleagues that we will not normally consider granting bail unless there are two sureties offering recognizances of £2,000 each". In this case, the detainee's sole friend in the United Kingdom was able to offer one recognizance of £2,000, but no other surety was available. In Case 50 (where a bail application was made without sureties) the Special Adjudicator stated that he had never heard of bail being granted by the IAA without recognizances, although he himself was willing to hear the application (in the event, the hearing was adjourned and the detainee was released on TA before the bail application could be determined at a further hearing). None of the 11 bail applications made without sureties, or with only nominal recognizances, was successful (see Table 3 for further information on the outcome of bail applications).[50]

It must be borne in mind that many asylum-seekers have no friends or relatives in the United Kingdom who could act as sureties in an application for bail. And, even in those cases where the detainee does have friends or relatives in the United Kingdom, such persons are most

---

[48] Paragraphs 22& 29 of Schedule 2 to the Immigration Act 1971, and rule 23 of the Immigration Appeals (Procedure) Rules 1984

[49] *Practice Direction on Bail*, issued to Adjudicators by the then IAA Chief Adjudicator in May 1991.

[50] However, there are some disparities in the practice of Special Adjudicators; in the four cases where bail was granted (Cases 6, 24, 36 and 42), the total recognizances accepted were £4,000, £4,000, £2,000 and £1,300 respectively, yet bail was refused in six cases where relatives or friends were offering total recognizances of £4,000 or more.

likely to be living on relatively low incomes: in many cases the friends or relatives will themselves be asylum-seekers on temporary admission, quite possibly living on welfare benefits alone. In such circumstances it is extremely difficult for would-be sureties to provide even minimal recognizances, let alone the large sums invariably demanded by Special Adjudicators.

In this context, perhaps the most alarming result to emerge from this study is that in 31 out of 50 cases (62%) there was no application for bail as the detainee did not have two relatives or friends in the United Kingdom willing and able to act as sureties, ie to provide sufficient recognizances. Among those who did not even apply for bail were two of the seven detainees ultimately recognised as a refugee and granted asylum. Indeed, it is abundantly clear that the application of this 'convention' by Special Adjudicators deters many hard-pressed legal representatives from making what they regard as pointless, but time-consuming, applications for bail, with the result that there is no independent review of the reasons for detention at any stage.[51] This is a violation of international standards, which require a "prompt" hearing before a court or similar review body *without which the person shall not be kept in detention.*[52] In other words, this review hearing must be *automatic*: it is not sufficient to require the detainee (or someone acting on his or her behalf) to initiate the process.

This lack of an *automatic* hearing before a court or similar review body also contrasts markedly with the United Kingdom's criminal justice system. Persons charged with a criminal offence punishable by a term of imprisonment may be remanded in custody pending their trial before a Magistrates Court or Crown Court, but *only* after a hearing before the court at which bail may be applied for. Furthermore, the Bail

---

[51] The problem is compounded by the fact that Legal Aid is not available to cover an application for bail.
[52] UN Body of Principles (Principles 4 and 11)

Act 1976 imposes a duty on the court to grant bail unless there are compelling reasons not to do so. In other words, there is an automatic hearing to consider the need for detention in each case, and a presumption in favour of release on bail.

The IAA bail process: lack of a "prompt" hearing to review detention
One further, and related, issue of concern to emerge from this study is that, even in those cases where an application for bail is made to the IAA, the applicant may spend a long time in detention before the application is actually heard. In the 17 cases where there was a bail hearing, the application was first heard after an average of 87 days (almost three months) in detention. In three cases the detainee had spent more than four months in detention by the time the bail application was heard by a Special Adjudicator or the IAT, and the four detainees granted bail spent an average of 138 days (4¹/₂ months) in detention before being released. There are clearly many reasons for these delays, including the restricted bail eligibility in "illegal entrant" cases and the need for legal representatives to find two willing sureties with sufficient funds available, but such delays are inconsistent with international standards, which require a "prompt" review of the reasons for detention by an independent review body.[53]

The IAA bail process: some general remarks
As a procedure for reviewing the reasons for detention, therefore, it is clear that the IAA bail process falls short of international standards in two principal respects: it does not provide a prompt and *automatic* hearing to review the reasons for detention; and, in "illegal entrant" and "deportation" cases, it does not allow for the detainee to challenge the reasons for detention *at any time* on his or her initiative. Indeed, in the majority of cases it does not provide any hearing to review the reasons for detention *at all*.

---

[53] UN Body of Principles (Principle 4 and 11)

Furthermore, in the minority of cases where an application for bail is made and heard by a Special Adjudicator or the IAT, whether or not the detainee is able to obtain his or her release is largely dependent upon whether he or she is able to offer substantial recognizances, rather than on an objective assessment of whether detention is necessary and for one of the reasons specified as legitimate grounds for detention by international standards. In Case 42, for example, the detainee had four applications for bail with only nominal or relatively small recognizances (£800 in the fourth application) rejected by the IAA, and was finally granted bail only after his sureties were able to offer considerably larger recognizances (£1,300) than in earlier applications; subsequently, the ex-detainee did not abscond and he was later granted asylum by the Home Office.

In this respect it is worth noting that, although in this study the Home Office and Immigration Service opposed every bail application, in seven out of the 12 cases in which bail was refused by the IAA the detainee was subsequently released on TA by the Immigration Service (and in two cases granted asylum), thereby placing a question mark over the effectiveness of the IAA bail process as a means of reviewing the reasons for detention. In Case 10, for example, the Special Adjudicator refused to grant bail even though two relatives of the detainee (one a British citizen) were offering accommodation and total recognizances of £5,000. Some two months later, however, the Immigration Service released the detainee on TA (ie without any recognizances being required), on the condition that he reside at his relatives' address. Similarly, in Case 45 the Special Adjudicator refused to grant bail even though two brothers of the detainee (both with asylum in the United Kingdom) were offering accommodation and total recognizances of £3,000. Less than one month later the detainee was released on TA and granted asylum.

In some of these cases, the granting of bail would have averted lengthy periods of detention. In Case 40, for example, the application for bail was heard and refused by a Special Adjudicator after 36 days of detention, but after a further 165 days of detention the detainee was released on TA by the Immigration Service. In each of these cases, the Immigration Service offered no explanation for the change in its position. As noted above, the fact that these detainees could be released on TA by the Immigration Service after such lengthy periods of detention strongly implies that the original decisions to detain them were mistaken, ie the original grounds for detention were fallacious, and yet in each case the IAA Special Adjudicator failed to recognise this when considering the application for bail.

It is also worth noting that, of the seven detainees who were ultimately recognised as a refugee and granted asylum, only two were released from detention as the result of an application for bail to the IAA. Two of these seven detainees did not apply for bail to the IAA (because they did not have friends or relatives who could act as sureties), two applied but were refused bail by a Special Adjudicator, and one was released on TA before his bail application could be heard.

However, setting these deficiencies aside for one moment, Amnesty International would not dispute that the Immigration Appeals Authority constitutes "a judicial or other authority under the law whose status and tenure shall afford the strongest possible guarantees of competence, impartiality, and independence" (UN Body of Principles). Given the existence of such a body, and the experience of Special Adjudicators in carrying out a review (however limited) of detention, it would appear to be a relatively straightforward step for the Government to make provision for a *prompt* and *automatic* review hearing before a Special Adjudicator in all cases. Similarly, in addition to this initial hearing to review detention, it would be a relatively straightforward step to make provision for all detainees to be able to seek, on their own initiative, a further hearing or hearings before a Special Adjudicator. And, if the granting of bail were to be conditional upon an objective assessment by the Special Adjudicator of whether detention is both necessary *and* for one of the reasons recognised as legitimate grounds for detention, then this area of detention practice could be brought into line with international standards.

Review of detention: the Government's response

In its formal response to the original edition of this report, the Government rejected Amnesty International's recommendation that each decision to detain be subject to scrutiny at an automatic review hearing before an IAA Special Adjudicator. In doing so, it once again cited internal Immigration Service reviews and the opportunites to seek bail from the High Court and IAA, or a writ of *habeas corpus* from the High Court. However, it failed to put forward any credible information or argument to rebut Amnesty International's conclusion that these mechanisms are defective.

With regard to applications for bail or a writ of *habeas corpus* to the courts, for example, the Government stated simply that "detention may also be challenged in the courts by way of an application for *habeas corpus*, or bail may be sought from the courts once a case is before them in an application for judicial review".[54] However, it did not address Amnesty International's concern, as expounded in this report, that the value of these mechanisms is nullified by their narrow scope, ie that they provide procedural and jurisdictional reviews only and do not allow the courts to examine the *merits* of the original decision to detain.

As on previous occasions, the Government maintained that "there is an extensive system under which bail may be sought" from the IAA.

---

[54] Letter to Amnesty International, dated 15 November 1994, from Home Office minister Mr Nicholas Baker, MP

However, other than conceding that "a small number of detainees are not eligible for bail" - in fact, approximately half of all detainees are affected by the restriced eligibility for bail in "illegal entrant" cases - it did not address Amnesty International's concern, as expounded in this report, that the value of the IAA bail mechanism is seriously diminished by the restriction on bail eligibility and the "convention" of IAA Special Adjudicators to demand substantial sums of money, beyond the means of most asylum-seekers' potential sureties, as recognizances.

In rejecting Amnesty International's calls for independent scrutiny of decisions to detain by means of automatic review hearings before IAA Special Adjudicators, the Government claimed that the cost of such a procedure "could be extremely high". It did not, however, produce any figures to support this claim. Assuming that approximately 1,500 asylum-seekers are detained each year, Amnesty International is confident that the implementation of such a review procedure would require, at most, two additional IAA Special Adjudicators (gross annual salary: £56,974 each). Even allowing for other related costs, such as administrative support, transport and escorts, Amnesty International is confident that the total costs associated with its recommended safeguards would not exceed £500,000 per year. Despite being invited to do so, to date ministers have not provided any information or argument to rebut this estimate.

While this is clearly not an insignificant sum, it is a fraction of the savings in detention costs that could accrue from the existence of such safeguards. According to figures released by the Government in the wake of the original publication of this report, it costs "just over £800" per week to hold an asylum-seeker in an immigration detention centre, and about £411 per week in a criminal prison.[55] As approximately 600

---

[55] Parliamentary Debates (Hansard), 23 November 1994, col 161 (written answer); and letter to Mr Robert Ainsworth, MP, dated 15 December 1994, from the Director General of the Prison Service. These cost figures were cited by ministers on a number of other occasions during November and December 1994.

asylum-seekers are held in detention at any one time (about half in immigration detention centres and half in prisons), these figures would suggest that the total cost of detaining asylum-seekers is as much as £20 million per year. On the basis of these figures, the maximum likely cost of implementing Amnesty International's recommended safeguards on detention (£500,000 per year) would be recouped if these safeguards resulted in a reduction of just 2.4% in the total number asylum-seekers detained each year.

However, the findings of this study of 50 individual cases suggest that the introduction of proper safeguards on the use of detention would actually result in a much greater reduction in the number of detainees. As described above, 44% of the detainees in this study were eventually released on bail or TA, after an average of 4½ months in detention, and did not subsequently abscond. Such a finding strongly implies that the original decisions to detain these 22 detainees were mistaken, ie there were no real grounds for their detention, and that they were held unnecessarily. Applying this finding across the board would suggest that, of the some 600 asylum-seekers detained at any one time, almost half are unnecessarily detained. Amnesty International believes that the introduction of proper safeguards on the use of detention would ensure that such cases are identified at an early stage - rather than after an average of 4½ months - with attendant savings in detention costs. On the basis of the cost figures provided by the Government in late-1994, Amnesty International believes that such savings could amount to as much as £8.8 million per year (and possibly much more).

In March 1995, the Government stated that "the overall cost of detaining a person in detention accommodation for which the Immigration Service is responsible is currently estimated at £540 per week".[56]

---

[56] Parliamentary Debates (Hansard), 8 March 1995, col 178, Mr Nicholas Baker, MP (written answer)

As of 31 March 1995, the Government has not explained the discrepancy between this figure and the higher figure repeatedly cited in late-1994, but even this lower figure would suggest that the total cost of detaining asylum-seekers is approximately £15 million per year. On the basis of this figure, and the findings of this study, Amnesty International believes that the cost savings accruing from the introduction of proper safeguards on detention could amount to as much as £6.6 million per year (and possibly much more).

Table 3: Applications for bail to the IAA

Abbreviations used: HO - Home Office;   IAA - Immigration Appeals Authority;   IAT - Immigration Appeals Tribunal;   TA - Temporary Admission

Case	Type	Bail granted	Comments
3	Illegal entrant	No	One written application made to IAA; heard after 77 days in detention; opposed by HO; bail refused by Adjudicator, despite relatives in UK offering total recognizances of £4,000.
6	Port case	Yes	One oral application made to IAT, at conclusion of appeal hearing; heard after 294 days in detention; bail granted by IAT, on total recognizances of £4,000.
9	Port case	No	One written application made (without sureties) to IAA; heard after 138 days in detention; opposed by HO; bail refused by Adjudicator. Subsequently released on TA (after 176 days in detention).
10	Illegal entrant	No	One oral application made to IAA, at conclusion of appeal hearing; heard after 110 days in detention; opposed by HO; bail refused by Adjudicator, despite relatives in UK offering total recognizances of £5,000. Subsequently released on TA (after 169 days in detention) to relatives' address.
14	Port case	No	One written application made (without sureties) to IAA; heard after 42 days in detention; opposed by HO; bail refused by Adjudicator. Subsequently released on TA (after 55 days in detention).
18	Deportation case	No	One oral application made to IAA, at conclusion of appeal hearing; heard after 173 days in detention; opposed by HO; bail refused by Adjudicator, despite friends in UK offering total recognizances of £4,500.
24	Port case	Yes	One written application made to IAA; heard after 118 days in detention; opposed by HO; bail granted by Adjudicator, on total recognizances of £4,000. Subsequently granted asylum.
31	Port case	No	One written application made to IAA; heard after 32 days in detention; opposed by HO; bail refused by Adjudicator, despite relatives in UK offering total recognizances of £7,800. Subsequently released on TA (after 78 days in detention), and granted asylum.
36	Port case	Yes	One written application made to IAA; heard after 35 days in detention; opposed by HO; bail granted by Adjudicator, on total recognizances of £2,000. Re-detained 7 days later, at conclusion of appeal hearing, and subsequently removed.

37	Port case	No	Two written applications made to IAA. First application heard after 28 days in detention; opposed by HO; bail refused by Adjudicator, despite friend in UK offering total recognizances of £2,000. Second application heard after 208 days in detention; opposed by HO; bail refused by Adjudicator.
40	Port case	No	Two applications made to IAA, both without two sureties. First (written) application rejected without hearing by IAA administrator due it "naming only one surety". Second (oral) application made at conclusion of appeal hearing; heard after 36 days in detention; opposed by HO; bail refused by Adjudicator. Subsequently released on TA (after 201 days in detention).
41	Port case	No	Two written applications made to IAA. First application rejected without hearing by IAA administrator due to it "naming only one surety". Second application (with two sureties) heard after 21 days in detention; opposed by HO; bail refused by Adjudicator, despite relatives in UK offering total recognizances of £5,000.
42	Port case	Yes	Five written applications made to IAA. First application rejected without hearing by IAA administrator due to "insufficient recognizances". Second and third applications (with nominal recognizances) heard after 47 days and 57 days in detention respectively; both opposed by HO; bail refused by Adjudicator. Fourth application heard after 76 days in detention; opposed by HO; bail refused by Adjudicator, despite friends in UK offering total recognizances of £800. Fifth application heard after 106 days in detention; opposed by HO; bail granted by Adjudicator, on total recognizances of £1,300. Subsequently granted asylum.
43	Illegal entrant	No	One written application made to IAA; heard after 98 days in detention; opposed by HO; bail refused by Adjudicator, despite relatives in UK offering total recognizances of £4,000.
44	Port case	No	One oral application made (without sureties) to IAA, at conclusion of appeal hearing; application heard after 82 days in detention; opposed by HO on grounds that applicant no longer eligible for bail (appeal having been heard); bail refused by Adjudicator, who accepted HO submission. Subsequently released on TA (after 209 days in detention).
45	Illegal entrant	No	One written application made to IAA; heard after 80 days in detention; opposed by HO; bail refused by Adjudicator, despite relatives in UK offering total recognizances of £3,000. Subsequently released on TA (after 104 days in detention) and granted asylum.
47	Port case	No	One written application made (without sureties) to IAA, but released on TA (after 76 days in detention) before bail hearing; subsequently granted asylum.

| 49 | Port case | No | One written application made (with nominal recognizances only) to IAA, but released on TA (after 32 days in detention) before bail hearing. |
| 50 | Port case | No | One written application made (without sureties) to IAA; heard after 74 days in detention; hearing adjourned at applicant's request, and no ruling made. Subsequently released on TA (after 110 days in detention), before further hearing. |

PLACE OF DETENTION & OTHER ISSUES

Place of detention: background

During the course of this study (August 1993 - March 1995), detained asylum-seekers could be held in one of three main immigration detention centres, Harmondsworth Immigration Detention Centre, Campsfield House Immigration Detention Centre, and Haslar Home Office Holding Centre (HOHC), or in one of several criminal prisons (the allocation of a detainee to a particular detention centre or prison being carried out by the Immigration Service's detention management unit). [57] On 21 March 1994, for example, out of the total of 651 asylum-seekers detained under Immigration Act powers, 136 were held in Campsfield House, 87 in Harmondsworth, 82 in Haslar HOHC, and 193 in 42 different criminal prisons (the remainder being held in police station cells or other places of short-term detention, such as Stansted airport). [58]

In June 1994 the Prison Service announced that, from October 1994, those long-term Immigration Act detainees not held in Harmondsworth, Campsfield House, or Haslar HOHC would be held in one of four criminal prisons - HMP Rochester (200 places), HMP Birmingham (65 places), HMP Doncaster (30 places), and HMP Holloway (30 places) - instead of being scattered in dozens of criminal prisons throughout the country. However, by November 1994 ministers were stating that this rationalisation of Prison Service accommodation would be completed "by the end of this year", and by January 1995

---

[57] There are also smaller Immigration Service detention facilities at Gatwick airport (The Beehive), Heathrow airport (Queens Building), Stansted airport, Manchester airport, and several seaports, but these are used for short-term detention (ie up to five days) only. In February 1995 the National Audit Office criticised conditions in some of these short-term detention centres. Also, in January 1995 the Home Office opened a temporary detention centre at Gatwick Airport, with a capacity of 45 places; a new, 125-place detention centre is due to open at Gatwick in the autumn of 1995.

[58] Source: Parliamentary Debates (Hansard), 20 April 1994, col 452 (written answer)

- when over 30 different criminal prisons were still being used to hold detained asylum-seekers - ministers were stating that this rationalisation would be completed "by the Spring of this year". As of 29 March 1995, asylum-seekers were still being held in at least 25 different criminal prisons, including Brixton, Winson Green, Manchester, Wormwood Scrubs and Wandsworth (see Appendix 2 for a full breakdown, by location, of those detained on 29 March 1995).[59]

Harmondsworth, near Heathrow Airport in west London, and Campsfield House, near Oxford, are both managed by the Immigration Service although the day-to-day running of the centres is carried out by staff of the private security firm Group 4 Total Security Ltd. Harmondsworth has a capacity of 95 places (including 14 places for female detainees) and Campsfield House has a capacity of 200 places (including 36 places for female detainees in a separate block).

Both centres operate a relatively relaxed and open regime: detainees have free association throughout the day and sleep in unlocked dormitories of varying size. At Campsfield House, which opened in November 1993 at a reported cost of £5 million, recreational facilities include a gym, several television rooms, a number of pool and table-tennis tables, and a small library with books and periodicals in various languages. However, educational facilities are limited to basic English language classes. Meals are taken in a communal dining area.

Haslar HOHC, in Gosport, is actually a Prison Service establishment staffed by prison officers, but is used almost exclusively to hold Immigration Act detainees (alongside up to 10 convicted prisoners who provide the prison's workforce, as Immigration Act detainees cannot be compelled to undertake prison work). It has a capacity of 150 places (for male detainees only). The regime is rather more controlled than at

---

[59] Source: Parliamentary Debates (Hansard), 31 March 1995, col 857-858 (written answer)

Harmondsworth and Campsfield House, as detainees are subject to prison rules and are locked in their dormitories at night and during staff meal breaks. Recreational facilities are similar to those at Campsfield House but in addition a well-equipped Education Department provides an extensive range of educational courses and vocational training.

As part of the rationalisation of prison service accommodation announced in June 1994, two wings of HMP Rochester are to be converted to hold Immigration Act detainees only, with a total capacity of 200. The first of the two wings (D Wing), with a capacity of 83, opened in July 1994 and, as of 31 March 1995, the second wing (E Wing) is due to open for Immigration Act detainees in May 1995. As with Haslar HOHC, the regime is more controlled that at Harmondsworth and Campsfield House, as detainees are subject to prison rules and are locked in their cells between 8pm and 8am; in D Wing, detainees are held in single cells (all with integral sanitation), while E Wing has a mix of single, double and larger cells. Detainees may take their meals in a communal dining area or in their cells, according to choice. At the time of an Amnesty International visit to the prison, in November 1994, the association area of D Wing included a TV room, a pool table and three table-tennis tables, and two pay-telephones. Other facilities - such as the hospital, chapel, and well-equipped education centre (where detainees can enroll for up to five hours' of education per day) - are shared with criminal prisoners held in separate wings.

Detention in criminal prisons

The 50 asylum-seekers in this study were held in each of the three principal immigration detention centres, Harmondsworth, Campsfield House, and Haslar HOHC, and in a number of criminal prisons. Twenty-eight of the detainees (56%) were held in a criminal prison for at least some part of the period in detention. In 22 of these cases the criminal prison was the first place of detention, and in 21 cases the detainee was held in a criminal prison for most or all of the period in detention. Prisons used included Canterbury, Wormwood Scrubs, Dover Young Offenders Institution, Holloway, Rochester, Wandsworth, Hull, Winson Green, and Pentonville (see also Appendix 1). This is at variance with international standards, which require that, insofar as detention of asylum-seekers occurs, detainees should "whenever possible" be held in facilities appropriate to their status, and not with persons charged or convicted of criminal offences.[60]

In Case 12, for example, the detainee (Mr P, an Angolan aged 22) was held for 112 days in the remand wing (A Wing) of HMP Wormwood Scrubs, in west London, before being transferred (at his legal representative's request) to Haslar HOHC. During this period, inmates on A Wing were locked in their two-man cells for up to 16 hours each day and, in the absence of a communal dining area, ate all their meals in their cells. As there was no in-cell sanitation the inmates had to undertake the daily ritual of 'slopping out'. Recreational facilities for the 270 inmates consisted of one television, one pool table, one table-tennis table, and a small library. The inmates included men charged with murder and other violent offences. At the time of an Amnesty International visit to the prison, in January 1994, A Wing was in a dilapidated and filthy condition, with rotting, foul-smelling rubbish (thrown from cell windows by inmates) littering the immediate surrounding area. Interviewed by Amnesty International, Mr P described "daily" incidents of (mostly drug-related) violence on the wing, and "frequent" threats of violence from other inmates. He broke down in tears as he described the constant fear and anxiety induced by his situation. Mr P was subsequently expelled to Angola (after a total of 216 days in detention), and Amnesty International is investigating reports that he was arrested upon his arrival there and subsequently imprisoned in the capital, Luanda.

---

[60] UNHCR ExCom Conclusion 44

Among those held in a criminal prison were six of the seven detainees ultimately granted asylum by the Home Office. In Case 7 the detainee was held for 145 days, first in HMP Bristol and then in HMP Pentonville, in Case 23 the detainee was held for 241 days in HMP Wandsworth, in Case 42 the detainee was held for approximately five weeks in HMP Canterbury, in Case 45 the detainee was held for 102 days in HMP Canterbury, and in Case 47 the detainee was held for 76 days in HMP Norwich. Two of the six female detainees were held in HMP Holloway for part of their period in detention.

One issue of particular concern arising from this use of criminal prisons was the isolation of small groups of asylum-seekers or individuals in some places of detention. In Case 4, for example, the detainee appeared to be the only asylum-seeker held in HMP Edinburgh throughout the 506 days that he was detained there, and in Case 48 the detainee appeared to be one of only two or three asylum-seekers held in HMP Hull for most, if not all, of the 113 days that he was detained there. These and several other detainees were consequently deprived of the support, both emotional and practical, available to those held in the immigration detention centres from the large number of fellow asylum-seekers (particularly those of the same nationality or speaking a common language).

In Case 23, for example, the detainee (Mr L, an Algerian aged 28) was transferred from Campsfield House to HMP Wandsworth after Immigration Service officials decided that he was "an exceptional suicide risk". At that time there was only one other asylum-seeker held in HMP Wandsworth, where inmates on the remand wing were locked in their cells for up to 23 hours each day and `slopping out` was still required. A regular visitor to the prison told Amnesty International that the atmosphere on the remand wing was at this time "very tense and threatening", with "a considerable amount of violence" among the inmates. In a letter to Amnesty International, written after he had spent over four months in HMP Wandsworth, Mr L stated:

"Today is my birthday and I'm in such a hopeless situation that I wish I was never born, and I did nothing to deserve it, I only wanted peace and to be free. This prison, without hope and faith to survive, is hell."

Mr L was subsequently released from HMP Wandsworth, after 241 days in the prison and a total 297 days (almost 10 months) in detention, and granted asylum by the Home Office. A medical examination carried out by the Medical Foundation for the Care of Victims of Torture found evidence of the torture to which Mr L had been subjected in Algeria.

Amnesty International and other agencies have not been alone in criticising the use of criminal prisons to hold asylum-seekers. In the case of HMP Pentonville, for example, the government-appointed Chief Inspector of Prisons, Judge Stephen Tumim, has stated that the prison is an "unsuitable" place to hold asylum-seekers, with "insufficient staff and facilities to meet their particular needs", while the prison's own Board of Visitors has expressed its concern that "an inner-city prison is an unacceptable holding place" for asylum-seekers.[61] Indeed, the Home Office itself has conceded that HMP Pentonville "does not provide the best environment for holding immigration detainees".[62]

More recently, the Board of Visitors of HMP Wandsworth has criticised the use of the prison to hold "deportation" case asylum-seekers detained under Immmigration Act powers. Concluding that "[Immigration Act] detainees should not be held in Wandsworth", the Board of Visitors has expressed its particular concern that:

---

[61] *Report on HM Prison Pentonville*, HM Chief Inspector of Prisons (March 1994); and *HMP Pentonville: Board of Visitors Annual Report for 1993* (March 1994)
[62] Letter to Charter '87, dated 25 April 1994, from Home Office minister Mr Charles Wardle, MP

"No one in the prison has any specific responsibility for [Immigration Act] detainees. Therefore no monitoring takes place. As detainees are effectively kept in ignorance by the [Home Office] Immigration Department of any progress in their cases, they become resentful and, unsurprisingly, draw attention to themselves by drastic action, usually food refusal. [T]he delays in processing these cases, whatever the outcome, constitutes an improper use of Prison Service resources and taxpayers' money".[63]

The current 'rationalisation' of Prison Service accommodation - whenever it is finally completed - will certainly represent an improvement on previous practice, as it should mean, for example, that single or small groups of asylum-seekers will not find themselves isolated among criminal prisoners. However, the continuing, and pre-meditated, use of criminal prisons to hold detained asylum-seekers is at variance with international standards.

Transfer to a criminal prison as disciplinary action
In this context, one particular issue of concern to emerge from the study is the Immigration Service's policy of using enforced transfer from an immigration detention centre to a criminal prison as 'punishment' for a real or perceived act of "indiscipline" or "disruptive behaviour". During the course of this study, four of the detainees were transferred from Campsfield House to a criminal prison on account of their alleged "disruptive behaviour", namely their role in the mass hunger-strike of February to April 1994 (Cases 8, 20, 24 and 46). In each case, the Immigration Service failed to inform the detainee's legal representative of the transfer. Moreover, in each case the detainee was not properly informed of the reasons for such disciplinary action, and was given no opportunity to put forward an explanation or defence of the alleged 'offence'.

---

[63] *HMP Wandsworth: Board of Visitors Annual Report for 1994*, (10 April 1995). On 29 March 1995, nine asylum-seekers were detained in HMP Wandsworth.

In Case 24, for example, the detainee was transferred from Campsfield House to HMP Winson Green, without notice and without being informed of the reasons for the transfer, the day after embarking on a hunger-strike to protest at his and others' incarceration. The detainee's legal representative was not informed of the transfer by the Immigration Service or Group 4 staff at Campsfield House, but learnt of the transfer from other detainees the following day. When she telephoned the Immigration Service at the port handling her client's case, a Chief Immigration Officer denied any knowledge of the transfer and it took several further telephone calls to Campsfield House to find out where the detainee was now being held. An Immigration Officer at Campsfield House subsequently confirmed to the legal representative that her client had been transferred after being identified as a "ring-leader" of the mass hunger-strike then taking place in Campsfield House. The detainee was subsequently released on bail by the IAA, and was later granted asylum by the Home Office.

During a visit to Campsfield House in February 1994, Immigration Service officials confirmed to Amnesty International that there is no internal disciplinary procedure at the centre and that, as a result, the only real sanction against "indiscipline" or "disruptive behaviour" by detainees is enforced transfer to Haslar HOHC, where the regime is more controlled, or to a criminal prison. However, in the absence of any formal disciplinary procedure, it is clear that the imposition of such 'punishment' by Immigration Service officials is not subject to any form of due process. This is a violation of international standards, which provide that detained persons "shall have the right to be heard before disciplinary action is taken", and "shall have the right to bring such action to higher authorities for review". [64] It is also in marked contrast to the situation in criminal prisons themselves, where The Prison Rules, made under the authority of the Prison Act 1952, set out 22 offences

---

[64] UN Body of Principles (Principle 30)

against prison discipline and the Manual on the Conduct of Adjudications governs a formal disciplinary procedure, including the right to representation, oral hearings, and a review mechanism.

Transfer to a criminal prison for medical treatment

In three cases the detainee was transferred from an immigration detention centre to a criminal prison for medical treatment. In Case 10 the detainee was transferred from Haslar HOHC to the hospital wing of HMP Winchester after he had spent 16 days on hunger-strike protesting at his incarceration. In Case 23 the detainee was transferred from Campsfield House to HMP Wandsworth after Immigration Service officials decided that he was "an exceptional suicide risk". In Case 44 the detainee was transferred from Harmondsworth to the hospital wing of HMP Rochester after making an unsuccessful suicide attempt.

The medical facilities in each of the three main immigration detention centres are rudimentary. At Campsfield House, for example, which holds up to 200 detainees, a nurse is in attendance between 9am and 5pm to treat minor ailments and dispense medication prescribed by a local doctor, who carries out daily visits to the centre, but there are no facilities or staff to deal with serious illnesses or injuries, whether accidental or self-inflicted, and at night there are no medical staff in attendance.

Such a basic level of medical facilities in the immigration detention centres is surprising given the particular medical needs of asylum-seekers, who may still be suffering the effects of imprisonment, torture, rape or other trauma in their own country when they arrive in the United Kingdom. These problems are often exacerbated by the debilitating effects of prolonged detention while their asylum application is considered, leading to anxiety, depression, and other psychiatric disorders. Since 1987 at least three asylum-seekers have committed suicide while held in immigration detention centres or criminal prisons, and there have been many suicide attempts. Three of the detainees in this study made unsuccessful suicide attempts (Cases 9, 11 and 44).

Principle 24 of the UN Body of Principles provides that "medical care and treatment shall be provided [to detainees] whenever necessary". While Amnesty International is not suggesting that detained asylum-seekers have been denied adequate medical care or treatment, it is clear that in some cases compliance with this international standard is only achieved by the contravention of another international standard, namely the requirement that asylum-seekers should, "whenever possible", not be held with people who have been charged or convicted of a criminal offence.[65]

Obstruction of access to legal representation

As described above, in four cases the detainee was transferred from Campsfield House to a criminal prison on account of his or her alleged "disruptive behaviour", while in three cases the detainee was transferred from an immigration detention centre to a criminal prison for medical reasons. In a further two cases (9 and 11) the detainee was transferred from one criminal prison (Dover Young Offenders Institution) to the hospital wing of another criminal prison after making an unsuccessful suicide attempt. In each case, the Immigration Service failed to inform the detainee's legal representative of the transfer, and indeed it is apparent that there is no formal mechanism requiring officials to so notify a detainee's legal representative.

In one case, moreover, staff at Campsfield House refused to tell the detainee's legal representative which prison he had been transferred to. In Case 8, the detainee's legal representative was informed of his client's

---

[65] UNHCR ExCom Conclusion 44

transfer by other detainees in Campsfield House. When he telephoned Campsfield House to find out where his client had been transferred to, a member of the Group 4 staff refused to say where the detainee was now being held and stated that it was "policy" not to disclose such information. Such action clearly has the effect, if not the intention, of obstructing a detainee's access to his or her legal representative, in violation of Principle 18 of the UN Body of Principles. In correspondence with Amnesty International, the Immigration Service has expressed its "regret" at the action of Group 4 staff in this case but, despite several requests, it has failed to provide clarification of any steps it has taken, or intends to take, to ensure that there is no repetition of such malpractice. It has also failed to explain what procedures exist to ensure that legal representatives are informed of the transfer of a detainee.

In addition, in a further six cases where the detainee was held in a criminal prison the legal representative reported difficulties in gaining access to the detainee to carry out interviews or discuss elements of the asylum claim. In Case 41, for example, prison officers at HMP Canterbury refused to bring the detainee to the telephone when his legal representative telephoned to speak to him. The principal difficulty in these cases, however, arose from the prisons' restricted visiting hours: in the case of HMP Hull, for example, legal visits are restricted to 1½ hours in the morning and 2½ hours in the afternoon, requiring legal representatives to make several visits to the prison to complete interviews. Furthermore, in some cases legal visits also had to be booked several days in advance. The imposition of such restrictions contrasts with the situation in the immigration detention centres: at Campsfield House, for example, legal representatives can visit detainees any time between 9am and 9pm, without having to make an appointment.

CONCLUSIONS AND RECOMMENDATIONS

The Immigration Act 1971 provides Immigration Officers with extraordinary and largely unrestrained powers to subject people seeking asylum in the United Kingdom to unlimited administrative detention. This 20-month study of 50 individual cases clearly demonstrates that the policy and practice derived from these powers violate international human rights standards in three principal respects: detainees are not properly informed of the reasons for their detention, and of their rights and how to exercise them; there is no automatic scrutiny and review of the reasons for their detention by a court or similar review body; and detainees are in many cases held with people charged with or convicted of criminal offences. The minimal safeguards on detention that do exist do not satisfy these international standards and are defective in practice.

The value of the right to apply to the High Court for bail, for example, is negated by the need for such applications to be preceded by an application for judicial review, a measure of last resort likely to be used at or towards the very end of the asylum procedure (if at all), and by the High Court's established reluctance to intervene other than in the most exceptional circumstances. And, as illustrated by the recent case of *Regina v Immigration Officer, Ex parte Khan and others*, the value of the right to apply to the High Court for a writ of *habeas corpus* is similarly negated by the narrow legal scope of this mechanism, which simply does not allow for scrutiny of the merit of the Immigration Officer's decision to detain the individual in question.

The value of the right to apply to the Immigration Appeals Authority (IAA) for bail is also severely diminished by the limitation on bail eligibility in "illegal entrant" cases, and by the "convention" of IAA

Special Adjudicators to require bail guarantees of £4,000 or more - sums beyond the means of most asylum-seekers. In practice, none of these mechanisms provides - let alone guarantees - adequate independent scrutiny of the merit of the original decision to detain.

As a result, large numbers of vulnerable people are subjected to prolonged periods of incarceration, without adequate explanation and without an effective opportunity to challenge the basis on which they are held, and often in conditions inappropriate to their status. This study shows that those so incarcerated include many people who will eventually be recognised as refugees under Article 1 of the 1951 UN Convention on Refugees, and strongly suggests that the average duration of such detention has increased significantly since the coming into force of the Asylum and Immigration Appeals Act in July 1993, with almost one-third of all detainees being held for more than six months. It also indicates that the debilitating effects of such prolonged incarceration induce a disproportionately large number of detained asylum-seekers to abandon their applications and return to the country from which they have fled, with an attendant risk of their becoming victims of human rights abuse in that country.

This study further shows that almost half of all detainees are eventually released on bail or temporary admission, a finding that casts grave doubt over the objectivity of Immigration Officers' decision-making and seriously undermines the Government's claim that decisions to detain are taken only where necessary and "only as a last resort". Indeed, taken together, the study's findings deepen Amnesty International's long-held concern that, in many cases, the decision to detain appears to be an arbitrary one, dependent more upon factors such as the availability of detention places and the Immigration Officer's demeanour than on an objective and considered assessment of whether detention is actually necessary. On the basis of its examination of a large number of individual cases (including those in this study) over a period of several years, the organisation firmly believes that in most cases detention is neither necessary nor for reasons recognised as legitimate under international standards.

Amnesty International is therefore calling upon the Government to carry out, in consultation with appropriate individuals and non-governmental organisations, an urgent and wide-ranging review of such policy and practice with a view to bringing these into line with international standards such as Article 5 of the European Convention on Human Rights, Article 9 of the ICCPR, UNHCR ExCom Conclusion 44 and the UN Body of Principles. In general, the Government should ensure that the detention of asylum-seekers is resorted to only for reasons recognised as legitimate under these international standards and *only when other measures short of detention will not suffice*. More particularly, the Government should ensure that, insofar as detention occurs:

- each decision to detain an asylum-seeker is made by a senior official of the Home Office Asylum Division, rather than an Immigration Officer;
- detainees are provided, at the time of detention or promptly thereafter, with a full, written statement of the reasons for detention (both in English and, if necessary, in a language which they can fully understand);
- detainees are provided, at the time of detention or promptly thereafter, with a written explanation of their rights and how to exercise them (including the right to obtain legal advice and assistance and the right to initiate a challenge to the reasons for detention);
- each decision to detain is reviewed as to its necessity and compliance with international standards by means of a prompt, and automatic, oral hearing before a Special Adjudicator of the Immigration

Appeals Authority (IAA);

- in the event that continued detention is authorised by the Special Adjudicator, detainees are able to initiate further challenges to the reasons for detention by means of such hearings before the IAA, *at any time*;

- detainees are held in specialist immigration detention centres in conditions appropriate to their status, and not with persons charged or convicted of criminal offences (unless so charged or convicted themselves); and

- detainees are given adequate access to their legal representative, relatives, UNHCR and other appropriate agencies, and the necessary facilities to communicate effectively with them at all times.

Amnesty International recommends that the initial, *automatic* review of the reasons for detention should be carried out by the IAA within seven days of the making of the decision to detain, and that further reviews of the decision to detain should be carried out by the IAA at regular intervals thereafter. The detainee and his or her legal representative should be permitted to be present and make representations at all such hearings, and it should be the duty of the Special Adjudicator to order the release of the detainee unless the Home Office is able to demonstrate to his or her satisfaction: a) that the individual in question is detained for reasons recognised as legitimate under international standards; and b) that other measures short of detention will not suffice.

In other words, there should be a presumption in favour of release and the burden of demonstrating the necessity for detention should be on the Home Office. In those cases where the Home Office argues that detention is necessary because the individual would otherwise abscond, for example, it must be required both to produce substantial, concrete evidence that the particular individual concerned is likely to abscond, *and* to demonstrate that there are no alternative means of making it likely that he or she will continue to appear at the asylum determination procedure. Such alternative means may, but need not necessarily, include having friends, relatives, or refugee agencies act as sponsors for the asylum-seeker by placing *reasonable* recognizances with the IAA.

In this context, Amnesty International would urge the Home Office to consider whether, in general, it would be more prudent to use detention only in appropriate cases of rejected applicants *at or towards the very end of the asylum procedure*, ie after the dismissal of an appeal by the IAA or the IAT, when the incentive to abscond is clearly much increased. Under existing policy and practice, and as illustrated by the 50 cases in this study, detention is currently used to hold asylum-seekers from the time of application (or very shortly afterwards), when no determination of the asylum claim has yet been made by the Home Office and there is, accordingly, little if any incentive to abscond (and when, indeed, the *disincentive* to abscond - in terms of having to live "underground" without access to the welfare and benefits systems - is very strong). In this respect, it is perhaps worth noting that the one detainee in this study who absconded (after being released on TA) did so only after his appeal to the IAA had been dismissed and arrangements had been made for his removal.

Amnesty International also recommends that all immigration detention centres be provided with appropriate medical facilities and staff to obviate the need to use the hospital wings of criminal prisons (or that adequate arrangements be made to use the facilities of local hospitals, when necessary). It further recommends that, in the event that it is deemed necessary to take disciplinary action against an asylum-seeker held in an immigration detention centre, such action be subject to due process. In particular, the detainee and his or her legal representative should be properly informed of the alleged misdemeanour, and should have an effective opportunity to present his or her response at an oral disciplinary hearing. Advance notification of the transfer of a detainee, for whatever reason, should be provided to the detainee and his or her legal representative.

Amnesty International recognises that the full implementation of these recommendations, particularly those relating to review hearings before a Special Adjudicator, would have significant cost implications. However, the organisation believes that such pragmatic considerations should never be used to justify a dilution of the Government's obligation to observe the various international human rights standards cited in this report. Moreover, the organisation is confident that the implementation of its recommendations would lead to a substantial reduction in the number of asylum-seekers held in detention, and that the attendant savings in detention costs would more than offset the additional costs associated with such safeguards.

On the basis of the figures provided by Home Office ministers in late-1994 (see *Review of detention* above), the total cost of detaining the 50 asylum-seekers in this study was approximately £640,000. Amnesty International believes that much of this cost would have been avoided if the organisation's recommended safeguards on detention had been in place. In particular, most of the total cost of detaining the 22 individuals who were eventually released on bail or temporary admission and did not subsequently abscond - £280,000 - would have been saved if these individuals had been released as the result of a prompt (ie, within seven days) and automatic review hearing before an IAA Special Adjudicator, rather than as the result of a successful bail application or a change of mind on the part of the Immigration Service after an average of $4^{1}/_{2}$ months in detention.

Appendix 1: Summarised case histories of 50 detained asylum-seekers

Abbreviations used:

DC - Immigration Service Detention Centre
TA - Temporary Admission
YOI - Young Offenders Institution

HOHC - HO Holding Centre (HMP Haslar)
IAA - Immigration Appeals Authority
IAT - Immigration Appeals Tribunal

HO - Home Office
HMP - Her Majesty's Prison
3C - Safe Third Country

Case	Nationality	Sex	Total time in detention (days)	Principal place of detention	Held in Prison[1]	Comments[2]	Outcome[3]
1	India	M	164	Haslar HOHC	No	Illegal entrant; no bail application as no friends/relatives to act as sureties; one application for TA refused.	Refused asylum; appeal dismissed; removed to India.
2	Sierra Leone	M	185	HMP Wormwood Scrubs	Yes	Port case; no bail application as no friends/relatives to act as sureties; one application for TA refused.	Refused asylum; appeal dismissed; removed to Sierra Leone.
3	Turkey	M	162	Dover YOI	Yes	Illegal entrant; application for bail refused by IAA; two applications for TA refused.	Refused asylum; appeal dismissed; removed to Turkey.
4	India	M	506	HMP Edinburgh	Yes	Illegal entrant; no bail application as no friends/relatives to act as sureties; two applications for TA refused.	Refused asylum; appeal dismissed; removed to India.
5	Zaire	M	278	Campsfield DC	No	Port case; no bail application as no friends/relatives to act as sureties; five applications for TA refused.	Refused asylum; appeal allowed by IAA; released on TA; HO counter-appeal to IAT allowed (and remitted to IAA); awaiting hearing of appeal to Court of Appeal against IAT ruling.

6	Cameroon	F	294	Campsfield DC	No	Port case; four applications for TA refused; released on bail by IAT.	Refused asylum; appeal dismissed; further appeal to IAT allowed (and remitted back to IAA); 2nd appeal to IAA dismissed; further appeal to IAT allowed; released on bail by IAT; awaiting re-hearing of appeal.
7	Lebanon	M	145	HMP Pentonville	Yes	Illegal entrant; no bail application as no friends/relatives to provide sureties; one application for TA refused.	Refused asylum and appeal lodged; released on TA and, following HO re-consideration of claim, granted asylum.
8	Zaire	M	101	Campsfield DC	Yes	Port case; no bail application as no friends/ relatives to act as sureties; two applications for TA refused.	Released on TA; refused asylum; appeal hearing adjourned; awaiting outcome of HO re-consideration of case.
9	Russia	M	176	Dover YOI	Yes	Port case; application for bail refused by IAA; two applications for TA refused.	Refused asylum; appeal allowed by IAA; released on TA; HO counter-appeal to IAT allowed (and remitted back to IAA); 2nd appeal to IAA dismissed; withdrew further appeal to IAT and made voluntary departure to Russia.
10	India	M	169	Haslar HOHC	Yes	Illegal entrant; application for bail refused by IAA; one application for TA refused.	Refused asylum; appeal dismissed; released on TA; removal directions set; absconded.
11	Angola	M	102	Dover YOI	Yes	Port case; no bail application as no friends/relatives to act as sureties; one application for TA refused.	Refused asylum; appeal dismissed; removed to Angola.
12	Angola	M	216	HMP Wormwood Scrubs	Yes	Port case; no bail application as no friends/relatives to act sureties; one application for TA refused.	Refused asylum; appeal dismissed; removed to Angola.
13	Romania	M	326	Dover YOI	Yes	Port case; no bail application as no friends/relatives to act as sureties; five applications for TA refused.	Refused asylum; appeal dismissed; removed to Romania.

	Country	Sex	Days	Location		Bail details	Outcome
14	Bosnia	F	55	Campsfield DC	No	Port case; application for bail refused by IAA; one application for TA refused.	Refused asylum on 3C grounds; 3C appeal allowed by IAA and HO then considered claim substantively; released on TA; refused asylum; awaiting appeal hearing.
15	Angola	M	389	Haslar HOHC	Yes	Port case; no bail application as no friends/relatives to act as sureties; six applications for TA refused.	Refused asylum; appeal dismissed; removed to Angola.
16	Ivory Coast	M	130	Haslar HOHC	No	Port case; no bail application as no friends/relatives to act as sureties; one application for TA refused.	Refused asylum; withdrew appeal on day of hearing and made voluntary departure.
17	Nigeria	M	108	HMP High Down	Yes	Port case; no bail application as no friends/relatives to act as sureties; one application for TA refused.	Refused asylum; appeal dismissed; removed to Nigeria.
18	Nigeria	M	231	HMP Bedford	Yes	Deportation case; application for bail refused by IAA; one application for TA refused.	Refused asylum; appeal dismissed; removed to Nigeria.
19	Nigeria	M	92	Campsfield DC	No	Port case; no bail application as only relative unable to provide recognizance.	Refused asylum; appeal dismissed; removed to Nigeria.
20	Zimbabwe	F	146	Campsfield DC	Yes	Illegal entrant; no bail application as no friends/relatives to act as sureties; one application for TA refused.	Refused asylum; appeal dismissed; removed to Zimbabwe.
21	Bangladesh	M	108	Campsfield DC	No	Port case; no bail application as relatives in UK unable to act as sureties.	Refused asylum; appeal dismissed; removed to Bangladesh.

No.	Nationality	Sex	No.	Location	Bail status	Outcome
22	Algeria	M	128	Haslar HOHC	No	Port case; no bail application as no friends/relatives to act as sureties; three applications for TA refused.	Refused asylum on 3C grounds; 3C appeal allowed by IAA and HO then considered claim substantively; released on TA; refused asylum; awaiting outcome of appeal.
23	Algeria	M	297	HMP Wandsworth	Yes	Illegal entrant; no bail application as no friends/relatives to act as sureties; two applications for TA refused.	Refused asylum; appeal dismissed; further representations made, with support of UNHCR and Medical Foundation, and HO agreed to re-consider application; released on TA, and granted asylum.
24	Zaire	M	118	Campsfield DC	Yes	Port case; one application for TA refused; released on bail by IAA.	Refused asylum; released on bail; appeal allowed by IAA; granted asylum.
25	Angola	M	172	Campsfield DC	No	Port case; no bail application as no friends/relatives to act as sureties; one application for TA refused.	Refused asylum; appeal dismissed; removed to Brazil.
26	Nigeria	M	154	Campsfield DC	No	Port case; no bail application as no friends/relatives to act as sureties; two applications for TA refused.	Refused asylum; appeal dismissed; removed to Nigeria.
27	Nigeria	M	202	HMP Canterbury	Yes	Port case; no bail application as no friends/relatives to act as sureties; two applications for TA refused.	Refused asylum; appeal dismissed; removed to Germany (where asylum claim outstanding).
28	Nigeria	F	111	Campsfield DC	No	Port case; no bail application as no friends/relatives to act as sureties; four applications for TA refused.	Refused asylum; released on TA; appeal dismissed; awaiting removal directions.
29	Nigeria	M	92	HMP Birmingham (Winson Green)	Yes	Port case; no bail application as no friends/relatives to act as sureties; two applications for TA refused.	Refused asylum on 3C grounds; 3C appeal dismissed; removed to Germany.

No.	Country	Sex	Age	Detention		Bail application	Outcome
30	India	M	115	Campsfield DC	No	Illegal entrant; no bail application as no friends/relatives to act as sureties.	Refused asylum; appeal dismissed; removed to India.
31	Iran	M	78	Campsfield DC	No	Port case: application for bail refused by IAA; one application for TA refused.	Released on TA, and granted asylum one week later.
32	Romania	M	145	Campsfield DC	No	Illegal entrant; no bail application as no friends/relatives to act as sureties; one application for TA refused.	Refused asylum; appeal dismissed; withdrew application and made voluntary departure to Romania.
33	Ghana	M	109	Campsfield DC	No	Port case: no bail application as no friends/relatives to act as sureties; one application for TA refused.	Refused asylum; appeal dismissed; removed to Ghana.
34	Ghana	M	128	HMP Wormwood Scrubs	Yes	Port case: no bail application as no friends/relatives to act as sureties.	Refused asylum; withdrew appeal before hearing and made voluntary departure.
35	Ghana	M	208	Haslar HOHC	No	Port case: no bail application as no friends/relatives to act as sureties; one application for TA refused.	Refused asylum; appeal dismissed; removed to Ghana.
36	Sri Lanka	M	35	HMP Canterbury	Yes	Port case: one application for TA refused; released on bail by IAA; re-detained 7 days later at conclusion of appeal hearing.	Refused asylum on 3C grounds; released on bail; 3C appeal dismissed and re-detained; removed to France.
37	Angola	M	252	Campsfield DC	No	Port case: two applications for bail refused by IAA; two applications for TA refused.	Refused asylum on 3C grounds; 3C appeal allowed by IAA and HO then considered claim substantively; refused asylum; appeal dismissed; released on TA; awaiting removal directions
38	Cyprus	M	72	Harmondsworth DC	No	Port case: no bail application as no friends/relatives to act as sureties; three applications for TA refused.	Refused asylum; appeal dismissed; removed to Turkey.

No.	Country	Sex	Ref	Location	Detained	Case details	Outcome
39	Ghana	M	207	Harmondsworth DC	No	Port case; no bail application as relatives unable to offer recognizances of more than £1,000: five applications for TA refused.	Refused asylum; appeal dismissed; removed to Ghana.
40	Peru	M	201	Campsfield DC	No	Port case; application for bail refused by IAA; three applications for TA refused.	Refused asylum on 3C grounds; 3C appeal dismissed; released on TA; following long delay in hearing of application for Judicial Review of IAA ruling, HO refused asylum claim substantively; awaiting appeal hearing.
41	Pakistan	M	48	HMP Canterbury	Yes	Port case; application for bail refused by IAA.	Refused asylum; withdrew appeal before hearing and made voluntary departure.
42	Congo	M	106	Harmondsworth DC	Yes	Port case; one application for TA refused; released on bail by IAA.	Refused asylum on 3C grounds; removed to France but "bounced back" and HO then considered claim substantively: refused asylum; released on bail; appeal allowed; granted asylum.
43	Turkey	M	156	HMP Norwich	Yes	Illegal entrant; application for bail refused by IAA; three applications for TA refused.	Refused asylum; withdrew appeal and made voluntary departure to Turkey.
44	Ethiopia	M	209	HMP Rochester	Yes	Port case; application for bail refused by IAA; several applications for TA refused.	Refused asylum on 3C grounds; 3C appeal allowed by IAA and HO then considered claim substantively: refused asylum; released on TA; appeal dismissed; awaiting removal directions.
45	Turkey	M	104	HMP Canterbury	Yes	Illegal entrant; application for bail refused by IAA; two applications for TA refused.	Refused asylum; appeal allowed by IAA; released on TA, and granted asylum.

46	Algeria	F	34	Campsfield DC	Yes	Illegal entrant; one application for TA refused; released on TA before becoming eligible to apply for bail to the IAA.	Released on TA; awaiting initial decision.
47	Turkey	M	76	HMP Norwich	Yes	Port case; bail application made to IAA (without sureties), but released on TA before bail hearing.	Refused asylum on 3C grounds; 3C appeal allowed by IAA and HO then considered claim substantively; released on TA, and granted asylum.
48	Turkey	M	113	HMP Hull	Yes	Illegal entrant; four applications for TA refused; released on TA before becoming eligible to apply for bail to the IAA.	Released on TA; refused asylum; awaiting appeal hearing.
49	Somalia	M	32	Haslar HOHC	No	Port case; bail application made to IAA, but released on TA before bail hearing.	Refused asylum on 3C grounds; 3C appeal allowed by IAA; re-refused on 3C grounds; released on TA; following long delay in listing appeal, HO agreed to consider claim substantively; granted Exceptional Leave to Remain.
50	Somalia	F	110	Campsfield DC	No	Port case; two applications for TA refused; bail application made to IAA, but released on TA before application fully heard.	Released on TA; awaiting initial decision.

Notes:

1. This column indicates whether the detainee was held in Prison Service accommodation (other than Haslar HOHC) – ie was accommodated, in contravention of UNHCR ExCom Conclusion 44, with persons detained as common criminals – at any point during the period in detention.

2. This column records the immigration status of the detainee at the time of application for asylum; the result of any application(s) for bail to the IAA and/or the courts; and the result of any application(s) for TA to the Immigration Service (prior to any subsequent release on TA or bail). The result of an application for TA is recorded only in those cases where there was an address to which the detainee could be released (provided by friends, relatives, a refugee community group, or a refugee agency).

3. In those cases not fully resolved, this column gives the position as of 31 March 1995.

APPENDIX 2: ASYLUM & DETENTION STATISTICS

Asylum applications & decisions, 1992-94

In 1992 the number of asylum applications declined noticeably from the previous year's high of 44,800, to 24,600, following the introduction in the latter part of 1991 of measures to deter and detect multiple applications. Of the 34,900 applications determined by the Asylum Division during the year, asylum was granted in 1,100 cases (3.2%) and Exceptional Leave to Remain (ELR) was granted in 15,300 cases (43.8%). At the end of the year, approximately 49,000 applications remained under consideration.

In 1993 there were 22,370 asylum applications (excluding dependants), of which 7,320 were "port" cases. The main applicant nationalities were Sri Lanka, the former Yugoslavia, Ghana, Nigeria, Turkey, Somalia and India. Of the 17,585 applications determined by the Asylum Division during the first six months of the year (ie before the coming into force of the Asylum and Immigration Appeals Act), asylum was granted in 1,275 cases (7.3%) and ELR was granted in 10,075 cases (57.3%). Of the 5,910 applications determined during the second half of the year, asylum was granted in 310 cases (5.3%) and ELR was granted in 1,055 cases (17.8%). At the end of the year 45,800 applications remained under consideration.

In 1994 there were 32,830 asylum applications (excluding dependants), of which 10,230 were "port" cases. The main applicant nationalities were Nigeria, Sri Lanka, Turkey, Ghana, India and Somalia. Of the 20,990 applications determined by the Asylum Division during the year, asylum was granted in 825 cases (3.9%), and ELR was granted in 3,660 cases (17.4%). Of the 16,505 refusals, 865 were made on "safe third country" grounds. As of February 1995, approximately 56,000 applications remained under consideration.

Sources: Home Office Statistical Bulletins 19/93 and 17/94; Parliamentary Debates (Hansard), 29 April 1994, col 346, and 14 March 1995, col 488 (written answers). Due to delays in decision-making, grants of asylum and ELR do not necessarily relate to applications made in the same period.

Asylum-seekers in detention, March 1995

On 8 March 1995, a total of 587 asylum-seekers (544 men and 43 women) were held in detention under Immigration Act powers. The following table gives a breakdown of these detainees, by nationality.

Angola	13	Libya	6
Albania	9	Sri Lanka	22
Algeria	58	Moldavia	1
Armenia	1	Morocco	8
Bangladesh	18	Mozambique	1
Benin	1	Nigeria	109
Brazil	6	Pakistan	26
Bulgaria	2	Philippines	1
Burma	3	Poland	1
Cameroon	3	Romania	9
China	19	Russia	3
Colombia	7	Sierra Leone	8
Dominica	1	Somalia	2
Ecuador	3	Slovakia	1
Eritrea	1	South Africa	3
Gambia	3	Sudan	2
Georgia	5	Thailand	1
Ghana	65	Togo	1
India	69	Tunisia	1
Iran	4	Turkey	25
Ivory Coast	6	Uganda	1
Jamaica	5	Former Yugoslavia	14
Kenya	4	Zaire	11
Lebanon	4	Zambia	1
Liberia	3	Total	587

On 29 March 1995, a total of 619 asylum-seekers were held in detention under Immigration Act powers. Of these detainees, 171 had

been in detention less than one month, 87 between one and two months, 171 between two and six months, and 190 had been in detention longer than six months. The following table gives a breakdown of these detainees, by place of detention.

Campsfield House	147
Harmondsworth	86
Haslar HOHC	79
Gatwick Detention Centre	35
Gatwick (The Beehive)	11
Stansted airport	13
Heathrow airport (Queens Building)	8
Dover port	6
Newhaven port	4
Birmingham Detention Suite	2
Manchester airport	1
Police cells	32
HMP Rochester	54
HMP Winson Green	42
HMP Brixton	11
HMP Manchester	10
HMP Wandsworth	9
HMP Greenock	8
Wolds Remand Centre	7
HMP Bristol	6
Brinsford YOI	5
HMP Exeter	4
Hindley Remand Centre	4
HMP Armley, Leeds	3
HMP Belmarsh	3
HMP Risley	3
HMP Wormwood Scrubs	3
HMP Birmingham	2
HMP Norwich	2
HMP Strangeways	2
Other Prison Service establishments	17
Total	619

Sources: Parliamentary Debates (Hansard), 15 March 1995, col 574, and 31 March 1995, col 857-858 (written answers)

APPENDIX 3: AMNESTY INTERNATIONAL'S POSITION & PREVIOUS WORK ON THIS ISSUE

Amnesty International is a worldwide movement whose work is based on the Universal Declaration of Human Rights and other internationally-recognised standards relating to the protection of human rights. As part of its work, the organisation opposes the forcible return of any person to a country where he or she might reasonably be expected to be imprisoned as a 'prisoner of conscience', or be subjected to torture, 'disappearance' or execution. It therefore seeks to ensure that governments take all necessary steps to identify such people and protect them against being returned to the country from which they have fled.

To this end, Amnesty International provides information to governments and to relevant individuals and organisations regarding the risks faced by asylum-seekers if forcibly returned to the country in question. It also monitors governments' asylum policy and practice to ensure that they are adequate to identify and protect persons facing such risks.

In this context, Amnesty International opposes the detention of asylum-seekers unless they have been charged with a recognisably criminal offence, or unless the authorities can demonstrate in each case that the detention is necessary, that it is on grounds prescribed by law, and that it is for one of the specified reasons which international standards recognise may be legitimate grounds for detaining asylum-seekers. The organisation calls for each asylum-seeker who is detained to be brought *promptly* before a judicial or similar authority, to determine whether his or her detention is necessary, ie other measures short of detention will not suffice, and in accordance with international standards.

Amnesty International takes this position because of the potential effects of detention in deterring individuals from seeking and obtaining asylum, notably that detention may impede the preparation of the asylum application, that the debilitating effects of detention may cause some individuals to abandon their application and return to their country of origin, even if this puts them at risk of human rights abuse, and that detention may increase the risk to individuals in a country where they are still in imminent danger of human rights abuse, by discouraging them from seeking asylum in a country where they believe they will be detained on arrival.

Amnesty International has long expressed its concern that Home Office policy and practice in respect of the detention of asylum-seekers falls short of the international standards cited in this report, and has repeatedly called upon the United Kingdom Government to amend such policy and practice. In November 1990 the organisation published a report, *United Kingdom: Deficient policy and practice for the protection of asylum-seekers*, making specific recommendations for change:

- detention of asylum-seekers should be avoided, and resorted to only where necessary and when other measures short of detention cannot be used;

- in so far as detention occurs, detainees should be given a full statement of the reasons for detention and should be allowed effective access to legal representation;

- the necessity of all decisions to detain should be reviewed as to their necessity and compliance with international standards by an independent, impartial, and competent review body within seven days of the initial decision to detain (and each 14 days thereafter).

These recommendations were publicly reiterated in May 1992 in a briefing, *Towards a credible asylum process: A model for fair and practicable procedures*, and again in November 1993 in a report, *United Kingdom: Unlawful killing of detained asylum-seeker Omasese Lumumba*. *(Omasese Lumumba*, an asylum-seeker from Zaire, was killed on 8 October 1991 while detained in HMP Pentonville pending a determination of his asylum application by the Home Office. In July 1993 an inquest jury found that he was unlawfully killed, as a result of the "use of improper methods and excessive force in the process of control and restraint" by prison staff. Amnesty International has called on the Government to initiate a public inquiry into his death.)

Since 1990, representatives of Amnesty International have also expressed the organisation's concerns and recommendations in a number of meetings with government ministers (most recently in September 1994), and in extensive correspondence with senior Home Office and Immigration Service officials. Regrettably, to date, none of the organisation's recommendations relating to the detention of asylum-seekers has been accepted by the Government.